Jesus' Abba

Jesus' Abba

The God Who Has Not Failed

John B. Cobb, Jr.

Fortress Press
Minneapolis

JESUS' ABBA

The God Who Has Not Failed

Cover design: Brad Norr

Library of Congress Cataloging-in-Publication Data

Print ISBN: 978-1-5064-0570-4

eBook ISBN: 978-1-5064-0571-1

The paper used in this publication meets the minimum requirements of American National Standard for Information Sciences — Permanence of Paper for Printed Library Materials, ANSI Z329.48-1984.

Manufactured in the U.S.A.

This book was produced using Pressbooks.com, and PDF rendering was done by PrinceXML.

Contents

Preface

1. Our Problem

For me, God is of central importance to life and thought. As a boy I found that my conviction fitted comfortably with widely shared belief. I did not agree with everything I heard people say about God, but the problem with "God-language" was not much different from other instances of disagreement and confusion.

Today the situation has changed. God remains of central importance for me. But I no longer find that belief to fit comfortably into my cultural context. On the contrary, many people are both skeptical that the word *God* has any reference and very uncertain what that reference would be like if it existed at all. In addition, the word now has a strongly negative connotation for many thoughtful and sensitive people, and I often find myself upset by how it is used.

If the problem were simply linguistic, we could solve it easily. Just use another term: *Creator, Goddess, Great Spirit, Almighty, Yahweh.* Using other names sometimes helps, but the problem is deeper. What has happened?

One problem is intellectual. From the outset of modernity, belief in the biblical God has been problematic. The biblical God is operative in both nature and history, whereas modernity, from its beginning, denied that God was a factor in what happened in the natural world. That is, it asserts that if you are trying to explain any natural event, you are not allowed to attribute any role to God.

At first, there was one exception. The world seemed so wonderfully ordered that it could not be thought of as coming into existence on its own or by chance. Most people assumed that it was created by an intelligent and powerful being, and did not hesitate to call that being "God." Scientists found that the world was governed by laws, so that the Creator was also the Lawgiver. Some religious people thought that every now and again the God who created the laws intervened and caused something to happen that did not obey them. Thus there were supernaturalists, but the default position was "deism," that is, the belief that God's only relation to nature was the one act of creation and the imposing of natural laws.

At the same time, everyone assumed that human beings were not part of the nature from which God was excluded. Opinions differed on how God was related to human beings. The devout could picture the relation as quite intimate, but the dominant culture encouraged the idea that God had created human beings and had also given them rules to live by. Unlike plants and animals, people might choose not to obey these rules. After death those who violated them were punished, whereas those who obeyed them were rewarded.

Deistic thinking still continues, but it has far less support than in the earlier period. It was deeply shaken by Charles Darwin's demonstration that the world we now know developed in a natural evolutionary way from a much simpler beginning. God was no longer needed to explain the remarkably complex and beautiful world we have around us; it could be explained by natural causes.

Equally important was that human beings are fully part of this evolving nature. If God is excluded from playing any role in natural events, then God is excluded from playing any role in human events. The default position now is atheism.

In the latter half of the nineteenth century, some Christians developed defenses against modern secular thought by affirming a fully supernaturalist Christianity. Here God plays a very large role. This dogmatic theism has contested the dogmatic atheism of the value-free research universities. For convenience I will call it "biblicist," since treating the Bible as having supernatural authority is a central feature.

Both sides became increasingly rigid, justifying themselves by the distortions of the other side. Those of us who grew up when the situation was more fluid and open have found ourselves alienated from both of these clearly defined positions. We constitute broadly what were once the mainline churches. For convenience I will call them "liberal" since they try to be open to what is becoming the dominant culture. Of course, many members are quite conservative in many respects, although few are comfortable with what I have called the biblicist position.

The greatest philosopher of the eighteenth century, Immanuel Kant, provided one solution for liberal Protestants. He wanted fully to support the work of scientists, but he wanted also to make a place for morality and religion. He distinguished between two types of thinking: theoretical and practical. Theoretical reason operates in the way that science has adopted, explaining everything reductionistically. Meanwhile, practical reason governs our lives, postulating personal freedom and responsibility as well as a God worthy of reverence. This dualism provides liberal Protestants a chance to accept evolutionary science without allowing it to affect their faith. It is the most common alternative to atheism and supernaturalist biblicism. Facts belong to science; values, to religion.

Unfortunately, like other dualisms, it has serious problems, because in actual experience values cannot be so neatly separated from facts. The act of worship loses much of its power when worshipers do not think that what they worship is factually real. I am one of many who have never been attracted by this solution.

Credibility has not been the only problem we theists faced. For many people "God" has become an offensive idea because so many terrible things have been done by his followers. I grew up believing that God was always good and loving. I knew that human beings, even those who worshiped God, had done some very bad things, but I supposed that this was an aberration and that we Christians had repented and were seeking peace and justice everywhere.

However, along with many others, I came to see history differently. In the name of God, Christians had persecuted Jews for most of Christian history. This persecution had reached new heights in what we considered a Christian country, Germany. True, the Nazis were not Christians, but they could show the continuity of their anti-Jewish teachings and actions with statements of Christian leaders, and the opposition to Nazi anti-Judaism on the part of Christians was weak.

I learned that in the century-long theft of the New World from its inhabitants, many Christian missionaries had played embarrassing roles. I learned that, indeed, even the more recent missions to Africa and Asia had often supported colonial exploitation of the people. Even the better missions were often tainted with the sense of Western superiority, and with condescension toward those to whom they were witnessing.

More generally, I learned that over the centuries the churches were usually allied with the rich and powerful. I learned that the enslavement of nonwhite races had been supported as God's will. I discovered that earlier members of my own family had written pious Christian books in defense of slavery. Even many of those leaders to whom we looked with admiration, such as Abraham Lincoln, had been racists. The Bible that seemed evidently to oppose such racism had been widely and successfully used to justify it.

In terms of our personal relations with God, I realized how legalistic we pious Christians had become. For example, I was brought up not to play with bridge cards. We played "Rook" with somewhat different cards instead. But on Sunday, all card games were forbidden. We played Parcheesi. Now this kind of legalism did me very little harm, but it illustrates a larger picture of "dos" and "don'ts" that can be very harmful and is clearly opposed by both Jesus and Paul. The legalistic spirit was destructively present in the suspicion of sexuality that led to complete silence about it in my home and to tight rules surrounding its expression.

Closely related to this legalism was the fact that Christianity, from a very early time in its history, had been patriarchal. That is, it had systematically supported the subordination and exploitation of women. The fact that God has always been addressed as male had played a large role, and feminists pointed out that the assumption of any kind of hierarchy as representing God's will was destructive of the full development of personal potentialities. Most images of the male God presented him as cosmic ruler and called for his rule of human beings as well. This was taken to authorize a male hierarchy in church and state.

In addition to all of this, we came to see that other cultures have developed religious ideas and practices that in some ways are superior to what has been accomplished in Christendom. Whereas, until recently, most Christians assumed that Christianity is the only truly advanced religion, we learned that it is one of several options. Its superiority is not, as I had earlier assumed, immediately obvious.

I could take some pride in the fact that as our consciousness was repeatedly raised on one issue after another, we liberal Protestants repented. That is, we tried to free ourselves from the ideas and practices that had done so much harm. We tried to reformulate our teachings. But our naïve supposition that belief in God evoked goodness in human beings was shattered. We saw that Christians had viewed God as the supporter of their prejudices more than as their judge. What was left, when we finished the reconstruction?

For many liberal Christians, the answer was "not much." Those who wanted to continue to participate in a community in which "God" was a central feature of liturgy sought ways to use the word that were free of the many destructive connotations I have noted. Paul Tillich helped some with his "God beyond the God of the Bible," Being Itself. Others have preferred to speak only of Mystery. Still others emphasize the nonrepresentational character of language, freeing people to use the word *God* without commitment to the existence or actuality of anything. All of these pointed to a God who does nothing. Appealing to such a God can do little harm.

I belong to this liberal group. But I am grateful for the second group, made up of Christians who have held on to the teaching of the Bible as they understand it even when the dominant culture turned against it. I have great hopes that those, within that group, who share my discomfort with its defensiveness, its rigidities, its dogmatisms, and its sometimes crude supernaturalism, will find their way to an authentically biblical understanding of God. But since I have never been part of that community, my path has been different.

I learned early in life that the Bible is the library of the ancient Hebrews and early Christians. It needs to be studied with all the critical tools that we use when studying other great literature. When this is done honestly and well, I have long believed, we find that the Bible is the greatest literary achievement of the human race and that keeping its wisdom alive is a matter of great importance. I have been saddened when I have found that some liberal scholarship has been so driven by reaction against supernaturalist views that it is uncomfortable with the strong claims I have just made for the uniqueness and importance of the Bible.

Much as I appreciate liberal Christianity and recognize it as my home, I am distressed by the direction it has taken. It continues to do many good things, and in its admirable aim to free itself from the many evils that beset our tradition, it has become harmless. But in a world that desperately needs strong and committed leadership and deeply dedicated followers, it has little to offer. It rarely challenges its members to devote themselves to God.

The focus of the liberal problem is the understanding of God or rather the lack of any consensus on this topic. I understand "God" as identifying the object of supreme loyalty. Some may use the term *God* in church with a different reference or none at all, but it is evident to the heirs of the Bible that those for whom "God" is the object of wholehearted devotion are not referring to the biblical God. Often they are more devoted to their nation than to what in church they call "God." Nationalism has been the most common and destructive form of idolatry in the modern world, both in our churches and outside of them.

In my view, the Bible is correct. We are called to worship one God, the God of the Bible. And today, more than ever before, we need this loyalty to the whole to unify our lives and our thought. Our many loyalties are blocking the action required to save humanity from utter catastrophe. We need wholeheartedly to give ourselves to working for salvation. This is hard to achieve without the belief in One who is, or relates to, the whole and is felt to be worthy of our total devotion.

2. My Proposal

My proposal is to think about God as Jesus did, and that should have some traction within both groups of Christians. Many in both groups take Jesus very seriously, yet neither group has devoted much attention to Jesus' own understanding of God. Clearly, Jesus was unstintingly devoted to God, and sought to be completely loyal. Perhaps if we could recover his understanding of God, it could evoke devotion from us also. Perhaps it would avoid the many traps that have brought the idea of God into such difficulties today.

To grasp Jesus' understanding requires that we make use of critical methods to distinguish Jesus' thought from the thought of others, especially those others who wrote about him. To do this we have to make judgments about the relative reliability for this strictly historical purpose of various writings. Biblical scholars have achieved considerable consensus on these questions. My intention is to build on that consensus.

Our earliest written sources are the letters of Paul. In them we learn quite reliably of Paul's own experience and about what was happening in some of the early, predominantly gentile, churches. But Paul does not give us much direct information about Jesus' teaching—he did not know Jesus before his crucifixion.

To learn more about Jesus' teaching, scholars turn to "Q," which stands for *Quelle*, the German word for "source," precisely because it is our best source for Jesus' sayings. It is generally supposed that oral collections of Jesus' teachings were put into writing before Matthew and Luke wrote their gospels, and these written sources account for some of the overlap in the reports by Matthew and Luke. Those who collected these sayings probably thought most of them were the actual words of Jesus, but modern scholars are more skeptical. Over time oral traditions begin to vary, and clearly some were modified in the course of transmission and new ones were added. Still, most scholars believe that we do have some authentic sayings. Certainly, the sayings collected in Q are our best source for reconstructing Jesus' own words.

Of the gospels we now possess, Mark is the earliest. Matthew and Luke seem to have had this gospel as well as Q to help them in the construction of their gospels. These three gospels differ in detail, but they give a similar overall picture of the sequence of events in Jesus' ministry. They are called "synoptics."

The fourth gospel, John, is deeply different. John is not interested in mere factual reports; it is their meaning that matters. What John's community has come to understand about the meaning of Jesus often appears in this gospel on the lips of Jesus. For the purpose of understanding the experience and beliefs of early Christians, and of inspiring later generations, John's gospel is invaluable. But it is not a source for reconstructing the words of the historical Jesus.

Another important question is about the language Jesus spoke. The New Testament consists entirely of writings in Greek. Jesus may well have known Greek, but it is highly probable that in his ministry with the common people of Galilee he spoke Aramaic. This is my assumption. A central thesis of the book is that Jesus thought of God as "Abba," the Aramaic word for father. I am suggesting that his understanding of God comes to expression in that word.

It is somewhat surprising that thinking about God has been so little shaped by the biblical texts and especially by Jesus' teaching. Those who emphasize that our scriptures have a different kind of authority from later writings should listen more carefully to scripture without forcing it to conform to what later came to be thought of as "orthodox."

My belief is that serious attention to the scriptures would free biblicists from some of their less attractive teachings, and this was confirmed for me by the experience of Clark Pinnock. He began as a fundamentalist, but was led by his belief in the divine authority of the writings to study them carefully. The results are to be found in "open theology," which I consider a particularly promising evangelical movement.

For most conservatives, including many I have classified as "liberal," some of five developments in church history have blocked appreciation of Jesus' own teaching. The first is the Vulgate, the translation of the Bible into Latin by St. Jerome. He was a fine scholar and although translation always involves interpretation, his work is excellent. It has influenced the later translation into Western European languages.

The problem I am noting here comes from just one of his decisions, one that profoundly affected Christian theology. He faced a problem with respect to one name for God, "Shaddai." For monotheists, proper names for God are awkward, because they reflect the earlier polytheism. Two proper names appear frequently in the Hebrew Scriptures. One of them is "Yahweh," and Jerome replaced this with "the Lord." The other is "Shaddai." As a conscientious translator, Jerome did not want to use "Lord" for this also. He chose to follow a practice already current, of replacing "Shaddai" with "the Almighty." The full expression is often "El Shaddai," and Jerome rendered this "God Almighty." This decision has led most readers of the Bible in the West to assume that the Bible views God as omnipotent. Many Christians consider any objection to this idea an assault on the Bible, although in fact it is intended for the sake of hearing what the Bible actually teaches.

The second problem comes from the creedal development of the early church. We can recognize the need of the church to settle controversies that arise within it through discussion at councils. We should appreciate their work and respect their solutions to their problems. Sadly, the creeds coming out of these councils were taken not to be just the best that could be done at the time but the inerrant and final solution to major aspects of Christian thought. Their authority supersedes that of the biblical writers and of Jesus himself. "Faith" is no longer understood, as by Paul, as trust and faithfulness. Instead "faith" came to mean the acceptance of ideas on the authority of the church, even, or perhaps especially, ideas people did not understand.

When Protestants criticized the church's claim to authority, they should have understood themselves as freed to reconsider the issues discussed at the councils in light of scripture. But they chose not to do so. And even within what I have called the liberal community, there are many who consider deviation from the classical creeds unacceptable. Fundamentalists, despite their prioritizing of scripture, seem just as committed to the traditional creeds as are Catholics, who explicitly give primary authority to the church. I am hoping that the time may finally have come when Jesus can again have priority over the Christ of the creeds.

The third major obstacle is giving special authority to Anselm of Canterbury, an eleventh-century theologian. In the New Testament account, Jesus is pictured primarily as a radical teacher. He regarded his message as supremely important for his hearers and for everyone; so he went to Jerusalem to confront the temple authorities. They decided to eliminate him and persuaded the Roman authorities to carry out the execution. Jesus might have escaped and gone into hiding, but he accepted crucifixion rather than flee or compromise. He did so for the sake of the people, even including the people who killed him. Anselm took the idea that Jesus died for the sake of others and transformed it into a cosmic tale about how God needs a sacrifice of such a scale that only God can make it. Although many reject his details, the idea that Jesus' death atones for human sins and is thus necessary for our forgiveness became entrenched in Christian theology. Since Jesus' teaching gives no support to the idea that God demands an enormous sacrifice in order to forgive people, followers of Anselm rarely give much attention to what Jesus himself believed and taught.

The fourth development in theology that blocks attention to Jesus is the adoption of natural law theory as the basis of Christian ethics. Jesus taught that "the Sabbath was made for people and not people for the Sabbath." In other words, any supposedly moral rules are to serve human well-being, not to hinder our expressions of love for the neighbor. Paul was consistent with Jesus and liberated believers in Jesus from Jewish law. But the church proceeded to replace Mosaic law with a complex system of law derived chiefly from Greek thought. This is a problem especially for Catholics, but it has spilled over into Protestantism as well.

The fifth development is actually recent. It is the attempt to identify some source for religious certainty. In my understanding, the Bible presents us a very uncertain world and does so in highly diverse ways. But one segment of Protestantism has declared that God prevented its writers from making mistakes. This blocks serious attention to Jesus' distinctive message, since every sentence in the Bible is equally inspired.

Catholics wisely avoided such bibliolatry but finally succumbed to the claim that under very special circumstances, the Pope can be infallible. His teaching is more authoritative than that of Jesus. In such a context, we cannot expect much serious attention to Jesus' message.

Both claims not only reduce interest in Jesus himself. They can only arouse incredulity and, at best, condescension on the part of most thoughtful people, including thoughtful Christians. Proclaiming infallibility as the basis for Christian theology spreads the incredulity to all the other beliefs now resting on the supposedly infallible grounds. The chances for Jesus to receive a serious hearing in this context are minimal.

My project is to bring forth Jesus' Abba as the God we can affirm enthusiastically and worship wholeheartedly. I believe that removing the obstacles I have listed will help. But it is important to recognize that Jesus' claim on believers can break through despite all sorts of theological obstacles. There are now, and have always been, thousands of people with highly varied beliefs who have loved Jesus and understood God much as Jesus did. Although some doctrines and ideas are damaging, I thank God that they do not always prevent devotion to Abba.

I have been encouraged to emphasize Jesus' distinctive understanding of God by a passage in *Process and Reality*, the *magnum opus* of my philosophical mentor, Alfred North Whitehead. He saw that most Western thinking about God was shaped largely by three factors. God was sometimes conceived after the model of imperial ruler, only incomparably greater. At other times God is thought of primarily in relation to giving and enforcing moral law. And another strain seeks the philosophic ultimate, such as Aristotle's "unmoved mover" or Thomas's "Being Itself." In Whitehead's view these approaches have not worked well. He notes, however, that

> in the Galilean origin of Christianity [there is] yet another suggestion which does not fit very well with any of the three main strands of thought. It does not emphasize the ruling Caesar, or the ruthless moralist, or the unmoved mover. It dwells upon the tender elements in the world, which slowly and in quietness operate by love; and it finds its purpose in the present immediacy of a kingdom not of this world. Love neither rules, nor is it unmoved; also it is a little oblivious as to morals. It does not look to the future, for it finds its own reward in the immediate present. (*Process and Reality*, corrected edition, p. 343)

It is noteworthy that at this point Whitehead does not mention Jesus.

He neatly bypasses the question of whether this understanding of God was original with Jesus or a product of his community. For all we know, Jesus learned how to think of God from his mother. To me this does not matter. We can learn about this fourth strand of thought only through Jesus.

I make a great deal of the fact that Jesus called God "Abba" or in English, "Papa." This is, of course, masculine. Because of this, I have held back on writing this book for many years. Few people believe that God is in fact gendered, and we have learned of the great damage that has been done by thinking of God as male. Several of the liberal denominations have worked carefully to rewrite hymns and retranslate scripture so as to remove the masculine bias. Progress in opening the doors of the church to the leadership of women has been astonishingly rapid. Some feminists have gone much further in rethinking the faith of the church.

However, on this point they have not been as effective, and the effect of neutering God has been disappointing. The worst example was replacing Lord with "Sovereign One." Better is switching to a biblical term like Creator. But a very important difference between Jesus and the Hebrew Scriptures of his time was the shift from monarchical language to family relations. "Creator" abandons that advance. Sadly, the English word *parent* lacks the relational connotations of "mother" and "father" that are so important here. Perhaps someday we can call God "Mama," but I think that, despite feminist victories in other ways, that day has not arrived. I have come to the conclusion that at this level, the use of Jesus' name for God, despite its being male, is an advance over the present situation for feminists as well as the whole church. I will wait no longer.

3. The Book

Chapter 1 of this book will talk about "Abba" and about Jesus. How is "Abba" different from "Pater"? What did belief in Abba mean to Jesus? What did Abba call him to do? What led him to his crucifixion? How are we to understand his resurrection, given his understanding of Abba? This direct discussion of Jesus' life with Abba is, of course, central to the book as a whole. Everything else hinges on this.

I am calling on us to follow Jesus in our thinking about God and our relationship with God. Some may suppose that this is what Christianity has always been about. It is partly true that Christianity has always been about God and our relation to God, but what believers have understood by "God" has very often not been what Jesus understood by "Abba." That is why I have written this book.

It will be difficult to return to Jesus unless we understand what happened in the church that intends to honor him in the highest of terms. Paul did understand Jesus—remarkably well. Abba was known and worshiped in the communities he established. But although that understanding never disappeared, and the words of Jesus were remembered and have moved many people, Jesus' distinctive thinking and feeling faded. People brought to the understanding of God what they learned elsewhere—sometimes from the Hebrew Scriptures, sometimes from philosophy. The new ideas took on a life of their own, and from early in the church's history, beliefs in God derived from sources other than Jesus played a greater role than Jesus in determining the understanding of God.

It is important to understand also how atheism became such an important part of the now-dominant culture. Much of the denial of God was justified, and attempts to defend some of the traditional doctrines that atheists are rejecting are convincing only to those who want very much to be convinced. I am not calling for that kind of theology. Instead, in chapter 2 and elsewhere I argue that the God that has evoked incredulity and hostility is not Jesus' God. If we affirm Jesus' Abba, the discussion about God is different and highly rewarding.

Critical historical study, including critical study of the Bible, has enabled us in recent times to clarify the various ways that "God" has been understood and also to articulate Jesus' understanding. This makes the thesis of this book possible. What is distinctive in this book (not unique) is the strong appeal to appropriate for ourselves the beliefs of Jesus that came to expression in his name for God: "Abba." Chapter 2 assumes the understanding of Abba developed in chapter 1, and describes how Christians compromised Jesus' own message and replaced it with less defensible ones. It is my hope that when we understand our history, we will rejoice in the renewed possibility of understanding Jesus' Abba and devote ourselves to the God of Jesus.

Chapter 3 tests Jesus' understanding of Abba against our individual experience. The experience I know best is my own; so chapter 3 is the most personal portion of the book. Its difference from most discussions of "religious experience" is that I focus on experience that is not typically considered religious.

These chapters can be read as my confession of faith, and those who find it sufficient may decide to skip to chapter 6. But I and many other believers in today's world have another need. Theologians sometimes call it "apologetic," although it is quite different from what we mean by an apology in ordinary language. It is a matter of giving reasons for holding to our faith in a context in which others think it is false or damaging. In today's context, as described in the first section of the preface and in chapter 2, my confession of faith may be tolerated as an expression of my idiosyncratic opinions. But most cultivated people will dismiss it as just that. They will assume they know that what I consider my experience of God can be explained psychologically. My apologetic is not apologizing for believing as I do, but rather claiming that those who dismiss my theism are mistaken. My defense is an offense, arguing that the assumptions underlying their modern understanding of reality are mistaken.

I have written about Abba realistically, that is, I have treated Abba as a real factor in Jesus' experience and in mine. Modernity declares that God cannot have such a role. Chapter 4 responds to this challenge with a counterattack on the dominant assumptions of the modern world.

The counterattack has two stages. Rather than begin with a critique of late modernity's a priori exclusion of God as a causal factor in the world, I take up a broader a priori exclusion. Modernity excludes subjects of any kind from playing a causal role in the world, accepting explanations only in terms of objects. Since Abba is a subject, if we adopt the modern position, the issue of Abba's playing a role cannot even arise. The first sections of this chapter argue that the rejection of the causal action of subjects is implausible and does not fit with the evidence.

However, by itself, recognizing the efficacy of subjects does not show that God plays a role. There are many who agree that subjects play a role, but think the only subjects are individual animals, including, of course, members of the human species. The latter sections of chapter 4 show that there are aspects of the public world studied by science that call for a theistic explanation, and that introducing such explanations is not harmful to science.

I noted in section 1 of this preface that the problem for people affected by modern, especially late modern, thinking is not only that of credibility but also that of desirability. Responding to this criticism is another task of apologetics, and I take this up in chapter 5. I hope that it is evident that understanding God as Abba will work against repetition or continuation of the crimes that Christians have committed in the name of God. But one question stands out. Does calling for devotion to Abba require undoing all the progress we have made in appreciating other great wisdom traditions? I think rather that the more we love Abba the more open we will be to appreciate and learn from others.

I indicated at the beginning of this preface that belief in God has never been more important. This is a historical statement. Faith in the biblical God has always been bound up with history, and today, what we have known as history is profoundly threatened. Our responses thus far have been woefully insufficient at least partly because serious commitment to the whole has faded.

Chapter 6 is about Abba and history. Loving the God of the Bible has been the major basis for developing historical consciousness. Today we need that consciousness as never before. But loving an omnipotent God, or a morally judgmental God, or an exclusivist God, or a God who demands sacrifice in order to forgive, can be harmful. Abba is none of those things. I believe that loving Abba is the best hope for the world's future, and loving Abba means working with Abba.

Abba cares much more about the future of the world than about who believes in him and who does not. We who love Abba will eagerly cooperate with those who do not, if they are working to save the world. But today we may rejoice that the leading voice in the movement to save the world comes from one who loves Abba: Pope Francis. It is my hope that my tiny effort to renew and strengthen the worship of Jesus' Abba will also build support for the great work of Pope Francis.

1

Jesus' Abba

In the Bible we find two major images of God, one, monarchical, and the other, familial. In the Hebrew Scriptures, God is most often imaged as "King"; whereas in the New Testament "Father" is dominant. Father has remained important for Christian understanding throughout history, and in languages that distinguish between an intimate "you" and a formal one, God is addressed with the intimate one. Although "thou" no longer has that connotation in English, its original selection did express the familial understanding of God rather than the royal one. Nevertheless, over time such ideas as divine sovereignty tended to play a larger role in Christian thought than the idea of paternal feelings. The latter introduces sentiment, and theologians rarely favor sentimentality. The shift began very early.

In the New Testament Jesus is never depicted as addressing God as King, and there is no indication that he spoke about God in that way. He always spoke to and of his, or our, Father. Nevertheless, in the Latin translation and in others derived from it, such as the English ones, we are told that his central message was a call to repentance, because the "kingdom of God" is at hand. It is all too natural to move from the idea that God has a kingdom to the idea that we should image God as King.

Since I am writing this book to encourage a return of our piety and theology to familial understanding, I will begin by arguing that Jesus' formulation as represented in the original Greek did not require this monarchical interpretation. The Greek phrase that we translate as "kingdom of God" is *basileia theou.* A *basileia* is a politically defined region. It could be a kingdom, and indeed most of them were, but the term does not include that as part of its meaning. If you suppose in advance that God is like a king, then the *basileia* of God will certainly be a kingdom. But if God is like a father, then his region or land will not be a kingdom. We might describe a father's *basileia* better as the family estate. Depending on the kind of father we are talking about, that might be governed in various ways. When we consider how Jesus talked about God, the answer is that it would be managed for the sake of all who lived there with special concern for the weak and needy. We have no word for this, but my proposal is "commonwealth." Jesus' message is that the "divine commonwealth is at hand." Everyone should reverse directions and join in this new possibility. There is no reason to think of the God whose *basileia* this is, as a monarch!

If this had been understood in the church, the Lord's Prayer would have ended as it does in Matthew and Luke with "deliver us from evil." However, many of us are accustomed to an added line that makes it fit with much other prayer and praise in our liturgies. I am accustomed to the addition: "For thine is the kingdom, and the power, and the glory forever." I have explained that the word translated "kingdom" is *basileia*, and this certainly belongs to the one to whom we are praying. By shifting here to "commonwealth," we could avoid distortion of Jesus' intention, but obviously this would not fit with the rest of the line. Early in the prayer we learn that we are to hallow God's name, but climaxing the prayer with a celebration of "power" and "glory" reflects the shift away from Jesus to royal imagery and sensibility.

I grew up with the idea of the kingdom of God and the celebration of God's power and glory in the prayer Jesus' taught us. I combined it in some way with the fatherhood of God even though my father was not like that. But I was glad to learn from scholars that Jesus himself had not wanted to evoke the monarchical sensibility.

Nevertheless, I continued to assume that, at least in the Old Testament, God was thought to be omnipotent, an idea that bothered me much more than the kingly language as such. Philosophically, if God has all the power, then we creatures have none at all, and if creatures have no power, then God's role of making them do whatever he wants does not in fact express much power. The whole idea is self-destructive. If to avoid the emptiness of strict omnipotence theory, it is explained to mean that God can control whatever he wishes, but gives some power to us to obey or disobey, the consequences still seem very disturbing. It is amazing that God does not wish to end some of the horrors of history or the extreme suffering of individuals! It is hard to combine God's permitting so much misery with the idea of his paternal love. I would not think highly of a human father who dealt that way with his children.

It came to me as a great relief when I learned from biblical scholars that the idea of divine omnipotence is not in the Bible. I explained in the preface that it was introduced into the translation to replace one of the proper names for God, "*Shaddai.*" There is nothing about the etymology of this name that suggests extraordinary power or control. I have been told by Jewish rabbis that the connotations might suggest "the breasted One." Accordingly, Jerome's assumption that "omnipotent" was an appropriate substitute for "*Shaddai*" clearly shows that by the end of the fourth century, the monarchical view dominated reflection about God. Once God is seen as "king," then to praise God is to praise God's power, and it would seem that if we put any limit on that power, we would be praising God less. When I have argued for a different view of God, based on parental images, I have been told that my "God is a wimp." For many, it seems, divinity is fundamentally characterized by the kind of power exercised by an absolute monarch, but this is not the way we evaluate fathers.

That the monarchical view of God has continued to be prominent is evident in the fact that so many prayers are addressed to Almighty God. When speakers do not want to repeat the word *God*, the most common replacement is "the Almighty." The resulting understanding of God has led millions to assume that God is responsible for creaturely suffering. Many who pray for relief and find none become deeply angry with God. Nothing has destroyed the faith of so many as the disappointment of the expectation fed by this language.

1. *"Pater"* and *"Abba"*

We have to wonder how Christians moved so easily from familial terms to monarchical images. It seems that the word *father* in English, and perhaps even more, *pater* in Greek, could have connotations that connect the two. In the Roman Empire, the *"pater"* had complete control of his household. He might be experienced by his children as a rather remote authority figure. In Western households through much of history the man has been the "lord of his home." If the term *pater* was heard in this context, then the return to monarchical imagery is not hard to understand. But these connotations should not be attributed to Jesus.

The New Testament was written in Greek; so the word used for father is *Pater*. Although Jesus probably knew some Greek, we can assume that he taught the common people in Galilee in Aramaic. Almost certainly his own life of prayer with God was in Aramaic. The Aramaic word for father was *abba*. Jesus spoke to God as "*Abba*" and taught the disciples to address God in that way. My judgment is that feelings that cluster around "*Abba*" are very different from the ones evoked by royal language.

"*Abba*" is, of course, baby talk. In many languages the first way we introduce infants to naming their fathers is by baby talk. Greek has such words, but they were not chosen for the translation. The translations from the Greek into Latin and later into European languages have used the more formal terms for the male parent. But in Aramaic *abba* was the only term for father. Jesus thought of God in a language whose earliest and primary connotations came from infancy. The normal relation of the father to the infant is one of tenderness and unconditional love. It was unconditional love rather than controlling power that dominated Jesus' understanding of God.

Perhaps my sense of the importance of using baby talk comes from my own experience. "Papa" is the closest English word to "*abba*." It happens that I called my father "Papa" not only as a child, but also as an adult. Of course, when I spoke about him to those who were not members of the family I sometimes said "my father," but I cannot imagine addressing him in any way other than "Papa." Now I have heard, and even said, "Father Almighty" often enough that it does not sound extremely discordant, but I cannot imagine speaking to, or of, God as "Papa Almighty." Language does make a difference.

Fortunately, in considering the importance of Jesus' calling God "*Abba*," there is some additional evidence in the texts. The Greek New Testament very rarely includes Aramaic words, but *abba* appears three times. The first is in Mark. He normally translates *abba* as *pater*, but on one occasion he keeps the Aramaic word alongside the Greek. Jesus is praying in anguish in Gethsemane (Mark 14:36). Mark writes: "Abba, Father, all things are possible for thee, remove this cup from me; yet not my will, but thine, be done." Mark seems to have felt that Father (*Pater*) alone did not communicate the depth of Jesus' feeling.

The other two occasions are in Paul's letters: Romans 8:15 and Galatians 4:4-7. The two passages are very similar. I quote Galatians:

> When the time had come God sent forth his Son . . . to redeem those who were under the law, so that we might receive adoption as sons. And because you are sons, God sent the Spirit of his Son into our hearts, crying "*Abba*." So through God you are no longer a slave but a son.

It is striking that at the moment of realizing the believers' filial relationship to God, their freedom from any lawgiver, the cry of the Spirit of Jesus is not the familiar Greek "*Pater*," but the Aramaic "*Abba*." Most of the members of Paul's congregations did not know Aramaic, but in this supreme moment of liberation, it was "*Abba*" that was spoken through them. This was apparently the case in Rome as well, a congregation Paul had not visited. (Note: I have been italicizing "abba" as a foreign word. But at this point I am appropriating it as my way of thinking, and speaking, of God. I will not italicize in future.)

2. Who Is Jesus' Abba?

Jesus was a Jew. That left open diverse possibilities for imaging and understanding God, but all of them were derived from the Jewish heritage. That heritage was from Abraham. Even today we speak of Judaism, Christianity, and Islam as the Abrahamic traditions, for all three communities worship the God of Abraham. This means that for Jesus, Abba is the God of Abraham.

This does not imply that everyone in these three traditions thinks of God the way he is portrayed in the stories of Abraham, for all three traditions are shaped by later developments as well. For example, in the Abraham stories, morality is noticeably missing, whereas all three communities highlight it. But Abraham's God was distinctive in a way that is still fundamental. He (and this God is envisioned as male) stands above and beyond all earthly powers and calls for a loyalty that relativizes all of them. Giving your final loyalty to anything other than this God separates you from the Abrahamic tradition. This demand for supreme loyalty is not affected by location in time and space, since God is not limited in that respect.

Like other Jews of his time and of all times, Jesus took this for granted; it was not a topic of discussion. But this shared conviction raised questions whose answers had immense practical consequences. Those who are devoted to the God of Abraham cannot give ultimate loyalty to anything else. The Romans conquered the Jews and ruled them, but they could not gain their supreme loyalty as represented in emperor worship. Rome made compromises with the Jews to pacify them, but even so, they continued to be a problem. There was an uprising in Galilee in Jesus' youth and two major revolts after his death. That loyalty to God trumps loyalty to any earthly claimant was a conviction Jesus fully shared. But he did not support the revolts to which this primary loyalty often led.

All the Abrahamic traditions not only identify God as the one supreme object of devotion but also share a development associated with Moses. For Moses, God is righteous and demands righteousness from those who worship him, and righteousness became central to the understanding of the Abrahamic God. In Moses, the continuing call for total devotion to God is accompanied by commandments explaining what it means to live in obedience to God's will, and what is known as the Mosaic Law spells out in detail the kind of life God calls for. Jesus' Abba is the Mosaic God of righteousness. For Jesus, as for all the other Jews, God is good and calls human beings to be good as well.

All views of the Abrahamic and Mosaic God attribute great power to him, but they differ in their understanding of this divine power. The differences have been sharpened for the modern world by the adoption of a mechanistic view of nature. If nature is mechanical, then God cannot be a factor within it. If God affects what happens, this can be understood only as a supernatural act that suspends the "laws of nature." If you approach the biblical stories in this way, you are forced to view them as full of the supernatural. And since the violation of the laws of nature is to most moderns a very unattractive idea, there is a strong tendency to dismiss the biblical accounts.

But, of course, it never occurred to the people of Israel that nature was like a watch and God like the watchmaker. On the contrary, they thought that God is involved in all worldly events, but for God to be active does not exclude other actors, so that the total explanation of the event includes both God and others. God is a factor in all that happens, but his role is often routine and easy to ignore, whereas in some events God's role is astonishing. Some of us today, who reject the mechanistic view, find this biblical approach intelligible.

Nevertheless, there is a tension within the Hebrew Scriptures between two ways of thinking. In one of these ways, nature in general—and human action in particular—is full of astounding occurrences. Alongside what we think of as ordinary creatures, various spiritual forces, of which some are demonic, play roles. In this ancient way of looking at things, events are products of the interaction of many factors, and sometimes the contribution of God leads to amazing results.

However, there are some passages that reflect another way of thinking, that is, that God sometimes displaces all other factors in the event. Consider the exodus story. Most of it belongs to the first way I have described. Moses engages in truly extraordinary demonstrations, but the competition between Moses and the court magicians shows that many events we moderns treat as supernatural can be effected by skilled magicians. This suggests that they may be masters of illusion as well as having extraordinary parapsychological powers. God's role seems to have been to enable Moses to outdo the others. But that does not mean that turning a cane into a snake and back again involves divine suspension of natural laws.

We find in the story of the crossing of the Sea of Reeds also an account that fits the first way. The God of Abraham worked through a strong east wind that pushed the shallow water away far enough for pedestrians to cross. But the mud mired the chariots that pursued them and as the wind died down and the deeper water returned, the Egyptian army was devastated. Here, God is an important factor, but he is not acting on nature against its inherent characteristics.

On the other hand, a second account is added that seems intentionally to emphasize the second way of thinking about God's actions. It is said that the waters of the Sea of Reeds stood like walls on either side of the Hebrews as they crossed (Exodus 14:22) and then crashed down on the Egyptians (as visually depicted by Cecil B. DeMille: Exodus 14:28).

My claim is that the dominant biblical view of God's working in the world is that he works in and through natural things and especially in and through human beings. God is very powerful but not the unilateral actor. I recognize that there are texts, and have cited one, that treat God's action as setting aside all other actors, but to call theirs *the* biblical view expresses a very unfortunate bias.

Advocates of divine omnipotence sometimes point to miracle stories of the second type as showing biblical support for their doctrine, but obviously between a supernatural act and omnipotence there is still a gap. Recognizing this, the advocates of divine omnipotence often assert that it is implied in the doctrine of "creation out of nothing." They are correct that creation-out-of-nothing would clearly be a unilateral act and is congenial to the idea of divine omnipotence, but in fact the idea of creation out of nothing is not found in the Bible.

The opening passage in Genesis asserts that all God had to work with was chaos. Genesis 1:2 says the "earth was without form and void." The clear implication is that the biblical author thought of God's creation more in terms of "order out of chaos" than as "creation out of nothing." Rather than finding its basis in the first verses of Genesis, the doctrine of creation out of nothing imposes on the biblical text ideas from other sources. The Bible does not support this doctrine.

The more general view in the Bible is that God is involved in every event but the sole actor in none. This view is consistent with most biblical passages speaking of God's action. It fits well with what we can reasonably judge to have been Jesus' understanding.

The shared acceptance by all the Abrahamic traditions of the Mosaic emphasis on the righteousness of God also allowed a great range of views of God and God's will for us. Out of the vast corpus of the law, some could emphasize the ceremonial obligations or the dietary laws. Others emphasized the Ten Commandments, which are silent on those topics.

Jesus stood in the tradition of the prophets. Beginning with Amos they denounced the focus on obeying rules and called instead for behaving justly. They were appalled that people would gather for religious feasts and ceremonies and continue to deal unjustly with the poor. True obedience to God was expressed in viewing matters from the perspective of the most oppressed. The widows and orphans were those who had the least status or security in the social system, and these are mentioned repeatedly in the prophetic literature.

That Jesus' spiritual Abba is the God of the prophets is clear in all his deeds and sayings. Further, his special choice from the great library of Hebrew sacred writings was the Isaiah scroll. In Luke the poem recited by Mary on the announcement of her pregnancy is a powerful prophetic utterance, the "Magnificat" (Luke1:46–55). Whether Mary is the actual source is anyone's guess, but it is not unlikely that Jesus imbibed much of his understanding of God from his mother. Certainly, prophetic ideas were prominent in Galilee.

The prophetic God whose concerns focused on the poor and oppressed could be represented in a variety of ways. The prophetic word was often harshly judgmental, and sometimes the announcement of a well-deserved punishment and the call to repentance could be associated with a frightening threat. But sometimes the emphasis was on God's mercy and the assurance of eventual relief. Sometimes the justice that was demanded was primarily an outward act, a way of structuring society. Sometimes the focus was on the heart, the inner life, and the motives of action.

Generally, the image of God's power is of control. I have argued that the texts rarely make God the sole actor in nature or history, but God's role typically appears to be to push in a particular direction, often decisively. On the other hand, sometimes we find expressions of divine intimacy and tenderness. Occasionally the language is drawn from relations in the family. Hence, Jesus' understanding has roots in the scriptures he studied. But nowhere in his sources do we find this intimacy and tenderness the central theme in the understanding of God. This was the revolutionary insight of Jesus: seeing God as Abba and understanding Abba's love as intimate and tender. Jesus' Abba is the God of the prophets qualified as love.

The word *love*, in turn, has multiple meanings. A king may

demand the "love" of his subjects, and while all Jews recognized the Mosaic command to love God with all one's heart, mind, and strength, that love was often understood to be fully expressed in obedience. The move from monarchical to familial language about God cut against this somewhat. But *pater* could still be understood primarily as one who expects from his children respect and obedience. *Pater* might be understood as one who always loves his children, but that love might be expressed in stern discipline accompanied by rewards and punishments. As I noted in section 1, the use of *pater* does not protect us from a move toward king and lawgiver.

The love of Jesus' Abba is not like that. The term leads us to think of the father of the newborn baby. Respect and obedience are irrelevant, as are discipline, rewards, and punishments. Abba's love is a deep feeling of unconditional commitment. It longs for reciprocal love. Of course it hopes for the future of the child to include virtue, but it is not lessened by misbehavior. Sometimes it seems to deepen when the child goes wrong. Jesus' story of the prodigal son expresses just this point.

Today many find the word *love* too hackneyed and vague; so they want something more specific, and the word *compassion* has come to the fore. It is an excellent word. Jesus' Abba is certainly compassionate, and Jesus embodied compassion. Allowing ourselves to feel the feelings of others is immensely important, and the new father will certainly be sensitive to the feelings of the baby. Abba's feeling the feelings of people is so complete that what we do to other people we are doing also to Abba.

But to describe the feeling of the new father primarily as compassion is not adequate, for there is a passion that goes beyond feeling the baby's feelings. It creates a bond that is life-determining. It includes the longing to nurture and protect. It is deeply personal and it includes commitment to the child and her or his future. It has what is now often described as "warmth." We need to affirm compassion, but we need to keep the more inclusive word *love*, remembering that for Jesus this is the father's love for the new baby.

The more we reflect on Jesus' understanding of his Abba, the more it can seem to us that he should have spoken of God, not as his father but as his mother. Mary seems to have played a much larger role in his life than Joseph. Certainly she has played a much larger role among his followers over the centuries. Was it not maternal characteristics more than paternal ones that shaped Jesus' understanding of God?

It may well be that, if the question had arisen in Jesus' day, he would have agreed, and one solution to the problem of gender language today would be to make the shift. One day, perhaps even soon, that shift may be possible for us. Already, we can pray, without offense, to the One who is Mother and Father of us all. But it was not possible in Jesus' day for him to call God "Mother," because that would have made people think that he was calling them to worship a female deity alongside the Abrahamic one.

Despite much recent experimentation with God terminology that is not masculine, there has been no real effort to replace "Father" with "Mother." Instead the move has been away from gendered language. In support of the important work of feminists, I have participated in this process. I have avoided pronouns for God altogether. I have supported the extensive work in removing masculine language from the hymns and prayers of the church.

However, I am not pleased with the result. This process has certainly raised the consciousness of millions of people about the fact that God is not a male and that males have no closer connection to God than females. It has had less effect on removing from the connotations of "God" the stereotypically masculine traits of laying down the law and controlling others. It has tended to depersonalize the individual's relationship to God; a neutered God feels less intimate. In short the admirable, and partially successful, efforts to overcome patriarchy have also blocked the expansion of the gains made by Jesus in shifting from monarchical to familial language.

After many years of neutering God in my language in support of feminist interests, I have decided in this book to re-gender God. When we talk about the effects of belief in God over the years, we communicate this more realistically when we make clear that in the Western imagination, God was male. For good and for ill, the God of Abraham, of Moses, and of the literary prophets was male. It is precisely feminists who have heightened our consciousness of this fact. I have decided not to conceal it by avoiding masculine pronouns.

Jesus' Abba was obviously also male, but Abba's character (in stereotypical terms) is more feminine than masculine. Perhaps if Jesus' description of God gains currency, the issue of Abba's gender will fade and pronouns of both types will become natural references.

3. What Did Abba Call Jesus to Do?

Jesus' deep intimacy with Abba was accompanied by a strong sense of Abba's call to do what needed to be done in his particular place and circumstance. The Jewish people, like most people everywhere, were absorbed in their day-to-day activities, but they were also torn between their devotion to God, largely expressed in following the Mosaic Law, and their desire to succeed in social and economic terms. They also felt a great tension between avoiding trouble with the Roman authorities and their Jewish commitment to put God first.

Jesus was clear that God must come first. That meant that the effort to succeed in a world that prized wealth and power must be put aside. For him that was not in question. He was also clear that the Roman emperor could not be obeyed when that obedience conflicted with the primary loyalty to Abba. But what, exactly, did that imply?

For most Jews there seemed to be two options. The first was to work with the Roman authorities to secure as much freedom as possible to practice the Jewish faith under imperial rule. Rome was pragmatic and willing to give a measure of autonomy to its subject people. From a broad historical perspective, the Jewish leadership had been remarkably successful in securing some unique elements of religious freedom within the Pax Romana.

Nevertheless, Roman imperial rule was exploitative and oppressive. Its system of tax collection corrupted those who participated in it and profited from it. The leaders who cooperated with Rome in order to get some autonomy also compromised and benefited from their compromising. For a purist like Jesus, this pattern of compromise and corruption was intolerable.

The recognized alternative was a struggle for political freedom. We would judge that there was no real possibility of gaining independence from the empire. The compromisers were right; theirs was the only practical solution. But many Jews refused this pragmatic perspective. Their history taught them that the God they worshiped was greater than any earthly ruler. They found in their scriptures promises of the restoration of the Davidic monarchy, representing both independence and real political power. In their communal memory, a Jewish revolt had thrown off the yoke of foreign empire and established an independent kingdom.

Furthermore, their scriptures spoke of a Coming One who would fulfill their hopes, the Messiah. The Messianic prophesies were vague and diverse, but some clearly implied that the Messiah would lead the people to military victory and the restoration of the Davidic monarchy. In Jesus' day, this was the most widespread expectation, and in his youth it had led to an abortive insurrection. Jesus saw that this form of hope would lead to self-destruction.

Jesus felt called to offer a third option. He saw it as the only alternative to compromise and destruction. To offer it was to play the role of the Expected One. But since "Messiah" meant to most Jews the fulfillment of the political prophesies, and his alternative was different, he could not simply use that term or make that claim. He believed that the only true fulfillment of Abba's promises was quite different from what the people in general expected.

Jesus' call was to take the call to be truly devoted to God with full seriousness. The overwhelmingly dominant culture could not be separated from compromise both with the aim for personal social and economic success and with existing structures of power. The mad effort to replace Roman power with Jewish power was not an answer. The God he knew as Abba was not the sort of being who would intervene in a war to remove one ruler and install another. The only answer was to replace involvement in the dominant culture with participation in a counterculture built on total trust in Abba and faithfulness to Abba.

In this counterculture, all know that they are loved by God and all love God. Also the participants love one another. And finally, they also love those who continue to live in the culture oriented to worldly goods and worldly power, even when they are persecuted by them. This belongs to the prophetic tradition, but it had not been fully envisioned before Jesus. It is both the fulfillment and the transformation of that tradition.

So what was Jesus' mission? It was to proclaim and to actualize this countercultural possibility. He called it the *basileia theou*, that is, the realm, or community, or commonwealth in which God's will is done. We are told in all the Synoptic Gospels that the heart of his message was: reorient yourself radically; the *basileia theou* is at hand.

What was immediately "at hand" was a small group of disciples that his hearers could now join. But he believed it was possible that the reality of such a community of authentic believers could spread and grow. He seems to have thought that even the temple authorities might see that this was the one way ahead. Whether he was ever optimistic that the people and their leaders as a whole would understand and adopt his third way we cannot know. In the end, it seems that he clung to hope without much expectation of success.

The *basileia theou* was the central topic of his teaching. He noted that "sinners" and outcasts were more likely to join than those who had some success in the present social order. Wealth was a special obstacle. He was emphatic that one who cares about wealth cannot serve God.

Some of his parables emphasized the extreme value of the option he provided. The *basileia theou* is a treasure for which one gives up everything else. To enter requires that we strip away our social conditioning as adults and return to the openness and eagerness of children. When those who are first invited to this feast refuse, the riffraff are called to join. The *basileia theou* is so small that it can easily be ignored, but that does not mean that it will fail to become a great force in the world.

I am interpreting the *basileia theou* as the actual community developing around Jesus. It was marked by an inclusive table fellowship in which all the distinctions of the dominant society were ignored. It welcomed whoever wanted to join, but they could do so only by breaking their ties with the dominant culture.

At the time, some understood the *basileia theou* eschatologically, that is, as having to do with the last things, the end time, and some scholars still do. It is my opinion that Jesus was opposing that view. He thought that looking for some dramatic act of God to usher in a new age was exactly what was wrong. What God did offer, God offered now. The *basileia theou* is already—now—at hand. Choosing to be part of it is an immediate possibility. Waiting for something else is a mistake. Indeed, expecting something else is a profound error.

Sadly, Jesus' own message is confused already in Mark, the earliest Gospel. When Jesus saw that the Jewish leaders would not support the alternative he offered, he foresaw the destruction of Jerusalem and Mark reports his prophesies of this destruction and indeed the destruction of much else. The Jewish revolts led to the predicted destruction of Jerusalem, to massive slaughter of Jews, and to banishing the remainder from their homeland. Jesus saw that this had become inevitable, and for Jews, the destruction of Judah was of such enormous importance that they could have easily regarded it as "eschatological."

Jesus certainly did not suppose that he knew when and how Jerusalem would be destroyed. No one could foretell that, but he may have specifically advised his followers to flee from Jerusalem when its end approached. While Mark, probably writing after the destruction of the temple, is likely to be accurate in recalling Jesus' prediction, his gospel interpolates an additional prediction of an entirely different kind (Mark 13: 24–27), which is quite unlikely to represent Jesus' own teaching. It jumps from a historical event to a cosmic one, whereas nothing else in the gospels points in this direction. Outside of the book of Revelation, there is very little of this kind of apocalyptic thinking in the New Testament. Sadly, those wanting to claim Jesus for beliefs that were truly opposite to his were given this toehold to do so.

One factor leading to Jesus' sense of special calling was his possession of charismatic gifts. His deep intimacy with God was accompanied by extraordinary powers. He was by no means the only "miracle worker" of his day, but he was an extraordinarily successful one. Moderns, of course, are uncomfortable with miracles, especially because the modern worldview can understand them only as supernatural, that is, as unilateral interventions of a divine being who is otherwise not active in the world.

The Jews of Jesus' day knew nothing of such a God or such miracles. They did know that some people had extraordinary capabilities and that some unusual events caused astonishment and wonder. These events seemed to express powers that were beyond the human even though they were embodied in human beings. Sometimes the power might be that of malevolent spirits such as Beelzebub. Sometimes the power might be of God.

Jesus' enemies did not dispute that he did wonderful things, but they suggested that his extraordinary deeds were possible because he was in league with evil spirits. One of Jesus' gifts was the ability to exorcise, or free people from demon-possession. He argued that the demons he cast out were allied with Beelzebub; so his powers could not be derived from that source.

None of this discussion makes much sense to moderns, but it was important to the reception of his message then, and the reality of miracles in the biblical sense is of significance even today. We can never have any certainty about which of the miracle stories are based on reliable memories and which are exaggerated or interpolated. But that many people came to Jesus in hope of healing and that some were healed is as certain as anything we believe about past events.

Jesus healed because he could and because he cared for people. But he primarily wanted people to heed his message. His miracles added to his authority and thus led to greater attention to his message. They also supported Jesus' view that if people gave themselves fully to the countercultural community he proposed, their essential needs would be provided.

Jesus' work as a healer had another consequence. It's clear that his fundamental message was formulated as a solution to a peculiarly

Jewish dilemma; so the mission to which he felt called was to the Jews. Nevertheless, he found that, through his charismatic powers, he attracted others. He explained to the Syro-Phoenician woman who asked him to cast a demon out of her child that his mission was to Jews, but her response was that, even so, he could also help gentiles. He relented and helped her (Mark 7:25–30).The gospels are full of incidents in which he is impressed by the healing faith he inspired in gentiles. Through this channel the door was opened to including them in the communities originally proposed as an alternative future for Jews.

4. Jesus' Crucifixion and Resurrection

Since Anselm, Christians have tended to focus on Jesus' suffering on the cross as the central saving act. If we do not follow Anselm, we are often told that we are not taking the cross seriously. Sometimes we are told that the only alternatives to Anselm are the rather lame moral-influence theory or the idea of Jesus ransoming us from the devil.

For a thousand years before Anselm, no Christian thought about Jesus' death in Anselm's way. And none of these options express anything close to the dominant view of the New Testament. Before we accept the limited choices we are so often offered, it is well to consider the New Testament's own account.

Paul is cited in support of Anselm, but only by distorting his actual views. It is true that he determined to "know nothing but Christ, and him crucified." But Paul never suggests that God demanded Jesus' death as a basis for forgiving us or even willed Jesus' suffering. It is not Jesus' suffering and death that saves us. For Paul, we are saved by our participation in Jesus' faithfulness to God. He marvels that this faithfulness extends even to death on a cross, and that Jesus died, not to benefit good people but sinners like us. Thus it is true that Jesus died for our sake. But for Paul it was his faithfulness, not the suffering on the cross to which that faithfulness led, that opens the way to our salvation. Of course, both Jesus and Paul knew that being faithful could lead to martyrdom.

What about Jesus? What do we learn from the Synoptic Gospels about his view of his coming death? The story may be summarized as follows. For some months, Jesus had a remarkably successful ministry of healing and teaching in Galilee. At some point he decided that he must take his message to the Jewish authorities in Jerusalem. In Galilee he had not been seriously threatened by the authorities, but it was clear to him and others that going to Jerusalem was likely to end in his death. Why did he go?

Since there is no explicit answer in the gospels, we do best to ask first: What did he do? His actions there were almost scripted. First, he chose a very odd way to enter the city and clearly planned his entry in advance in a way designed to fulfill a prophecy that was usually considered messianic. However, it was the prophecy of a humble messiah, one who enters the city on an ass instead of a stately horse (Zechariah 9:9). He was thereby making the claim that he was the one who fulfilled Israel's expectation, but he fulfilled it in a nonviolent and countercultural way. The planning was clear also in the presence of palm branches that had to be brought from Jericho for the occasion. Jesus arranged that his entrance would be acclaimed by his friends as an announcement to the public and the authorities of his claim to be the Expected One fulfilling the Messianic expectations in an unexpected way.

That his destination was the temple was also clear. If we follow Mark's account, on entry into the city, he took a look at the temple and then went back to Bethphage for the night. He returned to the temple the next morning and immediately threw the businesspeople out. From that point on he taught there intensively.

From his actions we may judge that his purpose in going to Jerusalem was to "cleanse" the temple. We can speculate as to why he judged this was worth risking his life. He must have decided that this was essential to his mission to provide a third way that would save Israel from self-destruction.

Why was it essential? To be a Jew in those days was to view the temple as the center of Jewish life. In fact, it turned out that Judaism could survive and flourish on the basis of the synagogue, but this was not anticipated by the people. To take a contemporary analogy, probably Islam could survive and flourish without Mecca, but for Muslims generally Mecca remains of central importance.

This center of Jewish distinctiveness was in fact corrupted both by close alliance with Roman rule and by exploitation of the piety of the people for the financial gain of a few. The corruption was apparent, and its association with Roman rule added greatly to the resentment of the people. To persuade the people to abandon hope of supernatural aid in overthrowing Rome would prove impossible unless the temple were part of Jesus' vision of countercultural faithfulness to God. It must be cleansed and put in the service of God rather than Rome. Jesus must take the desperate chance that the temple authorities could be persuaded to keep the temple pure. Jesus' success in gaining a real hearing in Galilee probably led to his hopes, however slight, that the Jewish leaders in Jerusalem might also listen and join him in proclaiming wholehearted response to God's love as the third way between compromise and violent rebellion.

He went daily to the temple to teach, but in a few days it became clear that he was not succeeding and that indeed the authorities were preparing to arrest him. He then faced the choice of fleeing or accepting execution. He chose the latter.

In Jesus' case we may be sure that he made every decision through sensitivity to Abba's call and guidance. In one instance we have the wording: "remove this cup from me. Yet not what I will but what thou wilt" (Mark 14:36). Abba did not want him to flee. He stayed and was crucified. By following this course, there was a better chance that his message would have some effect. For the sake of the cause, the alternative of countercultural communities of followers who loved God and neighbor, he accepted a miserable death.

There is every reason to believe that he would have far preferred to have won over the Jewish leadership. There is no reason to think that in this he disagreed with Abba. The idea that his mission was to die to appease the wrath of Abba was as remote from Jesus as devil worship, and its effect on the Christian world since Anselm has been poisonous. It is true that he died for our sake, meaning, for the benefit of all. This was the best choice left when persuasion failed. It is because he accepted crucifixion rather than fleeing and hiding that we have the chance to reject the values of the world and to live in the world as children of the all-loving Abba. Perhaps, in fact, this chance is more available because he failed to save Israel from the suicidal war that he foresaw, but he certainly did not want to fail!

How much Jesus foresaw of what then followed I certainly do not know. I feel quite sure that Jesus did not think his death would destroy his movement, nor did he think that his death would end his own existence or completely disconnect him from his followers. Jews thought of their great leaders as still alive and sometimes, as in Jesus' own experience, as appearing. The story of the transfiguration depicts Moses and Elijah as appearing to three of the disciples. Thus, in some important sense, it is likely that Jesus anticipated his "resurrection." He may have expected that, as his disciples broke bread together, they would experience his presence, and that, where two or three were gathered in his name, he would be with them.

In any case, what I rightly or wrongly attribute to his expectations occurred, and, as it occurred, the disciples recalled his prophecies. Their experiences were varied, and no doubt in the excitement of recovering the sense of his presence and the telling and retelling of how this happened, some events were imagined and others embellished. Probably the early accounts depicted Jesus very much as a spirit, without a physical body. Probably critics said the disciples had just seen a ghost and thereby minimized the importance of the experiences. Later stories heightened the physicality of Jesus and finally implied that his body had been resuscitated and eventually rose up to heaven.

That this was not the earliest understanding is clear from the fact that Paul never mentions it. Indeed, Paul teaches explicitly that the resurrection body is not the corporeal body, but a new body given by God, a "spiritual" body (1 Corinthians 15:44). For the many people who have had vivid experiences of recently deceased friends and relatives, the early accounts of resurrection appearances are easy to believe. Saying that the appearances of Jesus were probably much like the experiences of many others does not make them unimportant. Those who have had these experiences find them very significant indeed.

I will give one example that came close to home for me. Although psychological knowledge was much less developed in my youth, I can say fairly confidently that my older brother, James, was a victim of Asperger's syndrome. He was very intelligent but had no practical sense of how to function in social situations. My parents thought that if they treated him normally, he would become normal. This worked fairly well as long as he was in school. He graduated from law school. It was then apparent that he had no idea how to find employment or even, when he had to leave his dorm room, how to find a place to stay.

My mother left her husband doing his missionary work in Japan to make a home for James in Atlanta. After a few years, we made other arrangements that allowed her to rejoin my father. James engaged in routine work that we arranged for him without his knowledge. Someone made an appointment for him with a psychiatrist, who may have led him to understand his situation more clearly. Shortly thereafter he stepped in front of a train.

Needless to say, his suicide was a painful shock. I thought then, and I think now, he killed himself to relieve the family, and especially me, since I was the one with the most immediate responsibility, of the burden. I both deplored and admired his action, but above all, I hurt. I am sure our mother suffered most of all.

A few weeks later, she reported that James had come to her in a dream and assured her that all was well with him. She was profoundly comforted, as was I. For all of us this appearance was a matter of great importance, even though it had little effect on the way we proceeded to live our lives. Even if the appearances of Jesus had only been in dreams, they would have been immensely important to the disciples, and in their case, the appearances made a great difference in their lives and in world history.

Unfortunately, in the course of time, accounts of astonishing and reassuring experiences were replaced by radically supernatural stories. These are found especially in John, the latest of the gospels. For John the miracles function as "signs," that is, proofs of Jesus' divine status. Whereas in the first period the appearances reassured the disciples that they were right to follow Jesus and deepened their understanding of his message and mission, in the later period the resurrection was interpreted as supernatural proof of his divinity.

This process was much like the one noted above with respect to the crossing of the Sea of Reeds. In both cases, we are now confronted with stories that are intended to demonstrate that what happened was discontinuous from any historically possible event. But we can easily discern the earlier forms of the account, which, if you are not pre-committed to modern metaphysics, are quite believable.

In the case of Jesus, in the earlier accounts, his appearance and behavior do not suggest that the body that is present is the one that died on a cross. Today, when people have experiences, often including both sight and hearing, of one who has died, it does not occur to them that this means that the grave is empty. It was only because some Christians wanted to transform these wonderful meetings with the resurrected Jesus into proof of his divine status that the later stories turn the resurrection into a supernatural event.

If we are curious as to just what actually did happen, we can say with confidence that the disciples became convinced that in some form Jesus was once again alive. His work had not ended with his death. They were confident now that his teaching and his mission had all the importance they had attributed to it before his death—perhaps more. He truly was the expected one, the Messiah. That the resurrection appearances had this effect is hardly doubtful.

If we want to know in more detail how this change was effected, our best information is about the revelation to Paul. Whereas for the others the appearances of Jesus confirmed their faith, in Paul's case, since he had been persecuting followers of Jesus, the encounter led to a reversal of the whole direction of his life. In this one instance we have a recipient of a resurrection appearance making his own clear statement: he received a revelation of Jesus, calling him to preach among the gentiles (Galatians 1:12–16). Paul's own depiction of the context of the event and the secondhand accounts in the book of Acts are reasonably consistent. He was on his way to Damascus to persecute the followers of the Way, as Christians were then called. The revelation that Jesus *was* the Messiah totally reversed his understanding and his actions. The change in Saul was so profound that he took a new name: Paul.

Paul's reason for telling the story was not to claim supernatural authority or to set himself above others. The question was only whether his understanding of the implications of Jesus being the Messiah was derivative from the teaching of the other apostles. He is explaining that it is not. His realization of Jesus' Messiahship was independent of theirs and he did not consult with them about its meaning.

If we had only his account, I would be likely to interpret his experience of call to ministry as similar to my own. I had planned a career in government foreign service. But one Sunday, as I was walking to church, quite abruptly, I stopped. I realized that my vocation was to serve professionally in the church. It felt as though a decision had been made, but I had no sense of having made it. It seemed more like a revelation, and from this moment the future I anticipated was different.

Of course, my experience was more like the others' than Paul's in that the change of direction was minor. The change required of Paul was far more dramatic. He would serve the cause against which he had worked so hard and so harshly. It is not surprising that there were physical effects. We learn of these in the three accounts of the event to be found in Acts.

Saul is on his way to Damascus to persecute Jesus' followers there. The first account is as follows: "Suddenly a light from heaven flashed about him. And he fell to the ground and heard a voice saying to him, 'Saul, Saul, why do you persecute me?' And he said, 'Who are you, Lord?' And he said, 'I am Jesus, who you are persecuting . . .' The men who were with him stood speechless, hearing the voice but seeing no one" (Acts 9:3–7).

It is interesting that when Luke records Paul as telling the story, the account of what the others experienced is reversed. They saw the light but did not hear any sound. The third account tends to support this. We are left uncertain about what those who were with Saul experienced. Perhaps they just saw Saul fall to the ground and stand up temporarily blind. On the other hand, with full consistency we are told that Saul experienced a blinding light and that he heard a voice that convinced him that the one whose followers he was persecuting was in fact the Messiah. For my part, I take this straightforwardly.

A modern can easily explain the experience without reference to any involvement of either Jesus or God. But we are asking how the change in Paul came about. There is very little reason to doubt that Paul is telling us truthfully his experience. We may think a modern psychiatrist understands it better than did Paul. Perhaps. But if we do not share the modern metaphysics that knows a priori that many experiences are not what they seem, we may be inclined to take Paul seriously.

Paul also lists the resurrection appearances prior to his. Presumably he assumed they were more or less similar to his. This seems plausible to me. He omitted many of the stories later reported in the gospels. These omissions do not prove that there were in fact no other resurrection appearances. But they make clear that many of the stories of resurrection encounters that we find in the gospels were not in wide circulation at the time Paul wrote or, if they were, did not seem authentic to Paul. In all probability there were embellishments over the decades before the gospels were written. But that Jesus appeared to Paul and others is, for me, not in doubt.

Our focus is on Abba. How was Abba involved in Jesus' resurrection? Sometimes we are told that "Jesus rose." Sometimes we are told that "God raised Jesus." This ambiguity is like the ambiguity in the healing stories. Sometimes we are told that Jesus healed people—sometimes Jesus says that the faith of the individual healed her or him. The New Testament does not worry about these differences. In the healing stories certainly Abba is at work; certainly Jesus is at work; certainly the attitude of the one seeking healing is important. Similarly, there would be no resurrection without Abba's involvement, and there would be no resurrection without Jesus' involvement. Abba acts in and through creatures, especially humans, and in a special way through people who align themselves with Abba's call.

2

What Happened to Abba in Western History?

Over time it often happens that some aspects of a great movement are lost or obscured. That this happened in Christianity is no secret. There are frequent efforts to recover the earlier qualities, and this book is another such effort.

To have any chance of success, it is important to examine when and how the loss occurred. I am emphasizing the loss of the unique understanding of God that Jesus introduced into history. If it had no effect among his followers, then it would be foolhardy to suggest that we could learn and embody it now. But it deeply informed the early Christian communities, and that gives me hope that it could inform us today. In this first section I examine the early churches to see how the relation to Abba developed even when the language was different.

1. Abba as the Spirit in Paul's Churches

After what Paul considered Jesus' final appearance, that is, Jesus' appearance to him, Jesus' presence continued to be felt. The earliest and clearest testimony to this is in Paul. A fundamental characteristic of his congregations was the experience of the Spirit. This could be thought of as the Spirit of God, but Paul never separated it from Jesus. The God of whom he speaks is emphatically the Abba of Jesus. When he speaks of the Spirit of God, Jesus is already implied. Sometimes he speaks of the Spirit of the Son. Elsewhere he explicitly identifies the Spirit with the Lord, who is certainly the resurrected Jesus. Always he was speaking of the Spirit that was so powerfully felt by the participants in his congregations that its reality was never in doubt.

Because this was the Spirit of Jesus and of Jesus' Abba, it was also, first and foremost the Spirit of love, and this was the love described in chapter 1 as illustrated in a father's feeling for his infant child. It broke through all social distinctions. The exclusion of these from Jesus' *basileia theou* is clear from Jesus' actions and message. Paul makes it explicit. Paul understands believers to live *en Christo*, that is, in the Messiah, which means also in Jesus. Paul asserts that in Christ "there is neither Jew nor Gentile, neither slave nor free, neither male nor female" (Galatians 3:28).

Furthermore, morality was transcended. Loving response to God's love and participation in the faithfulness of Jesus leave moral judgments behind. For Jesus, the law is made for people, not people for the law. When the law forbids what is needed for actual human well-being, it is to be ignored. The only absolute law is the law of love. Paul for all time clarifies the nature of freedom from the law and how, for the sake of true righteousness, love transcends all human rules. The communities that understood this were radically countercultural places in which Abba's love was felt, reciprocated, and shared.

Paul is often thought of as the apostle of *pistis* rather than *agape.* When *pistis* is translated as "faith" there can be a significant difference, but Paul's meaning is much broader, and it is better captured in "faithfulness." Paul marvels at Jesus' faithfulness and calls us to participate in it. Since Jesus' faithfulness is a loving response to the love of Abba, our participation in that faithfulness is also a matter of love. Contrasting Paul's concern for *pistis* to love does not make sense.

Paul includes a beautiful poem about love, the thirteenth chapter of 1 Corinthians. This takes faith and love as quite distinct, celebrates both, and claims that love is the most important. Here "faith" means the sort of belief and trust that allowed marvelous healings to occur. The poem asserts that even if this faith is so strong that it can move mountains, it is worthless without love. Paul clearly agrees. Here and elsewhere he recognizes that marvels occur and that the Spirit in the church supports these. People gifted in spiritual healing and in prophecy make important contributions to the church. But he does not put them forward as proofs of the truth of the message. They are byproducts to be celebrated, but they do not display the *pistis* that saves us. That *pistis* is inseparable from love.

Paul's communities are true embodiments of what Jesus called the *basileia theou*. Paul used that term to refer to Abba's reign in heaven. Jesus' focus on what is possible here and now is qualified by Paul. Despite his overwhelming focus on what is happening in these communities, he sometimes suggests that the importance of all this depends on the life beyond death for which it prepares us.

For Jesus, communities of this sort were the alternative to the self-destruction of Israel, and in fact Paul's churches were of immense historical importance. It was largely through them that the legacy of Jesus' countercultural communities became important in world history. But this historical context played no role in Paul. In this respect, his relocation of the *basileia theou* in heaven is an unfortunate change that has shaped much of Christianity ever since. Jesus certainly assumed that life beyond this world was real, but Jesus' Abba loves concrete people in their concrete situation in this world. What happens in this world is immensely important. Our mission here and now is determined by the current personal and historical situation. The church is healthiest when Jesus' weighting of importance dominates.

The difference between Paul and Jesus may result from the fact that within the Roman Empire, realistically, citizens could make little difference of a historical sort. In contrast, Jesus seems to have thought there was a possibility that Israel could avoid suicidal actions. Where people are powerless to affect the larger context or the future, they rightly concentrate on what is really at hand. Since a larger context certainly adds to importance, the context of life beyond death could serve Paul well. Indeed, it is somewhat surprising that, despite one outburst with regard to its importance, he rarely discusses it.

2. Did Abba Become Mary in the Medieval Church?

When we view later periods of the church, it becomes more difficult to find the effectiveness of Jesus' teaching about God. The change began soon after the first generation of Christians. This is not the place to examine the history in detail; so we will jump to the next period of Christianity, the Middle Ages, in which the church had moved from its marginal beginning to become the most important institution in society. This period lasted for a thousand years, during which Christianity created a great civilization. Since moderns are often cavalierly dismissive of it, I want to give some emphasis to the church's achievements before acknowledging that Abba was too little appreciated.

Already in the early centuries, it became clear that the Christian churches, almost in spite of themselves, were a world-changing phenomenon. To have communities that looked for meaning and direction beyond the empire and its rulers was deeply troubling to political authorities. They tried to stamp this out, or at least keep it within narrow bounds, but the churches grew. Whether this contributed to the collapse of the Western empire is unclear. But while the empire imploded the church thrived.

In the following millennium, the church engaged in an experiment on a vast scale: namely, a society that did not concentrate all power in one person or institution. Political power and spiritual-cultural power were separated. Both were held to be subordinate to God, but because the church was more explicitly representative of God, it tended to dominate. Political power was distributed among kings and, within kingdoms, among nobles of various ranks. Some cities had independent charters. Merchants, artisans, and professionals had considerable freedom to govern themselves. Slavery was abolished, and although peasants were exploited, they also had their rights. For a thousand chaotic years, this was Christendom, the massive historical result of countercultural communities that denied the empire their ultimate loyalty. The church provided its unity without military force. Of course, within Christendom political rulers fought one another, but compared with the preceding and succeeding periods, the role of violence was moderate. Before criticizing the Middle Ages and the church that gave it its distinctive character, it is important to recognize the quite amazing achievements of the period.

It is truly astonishing how ignorant the modern world has been of its predecessor. This ignorance is partly willful. The only justification of modern secularism is that Christendom was worse. Hence a millennium of rich culture and history is often dismissed as "the dark ages."

It is, of course, true that in the Roman Empire, based on a slave society, an elite had the leisure to develop a high culture with many magnificent expressions in literature, architecture, and philosophy.

The collapse of empire destroyed *that* elite. If we measure cultures by the achievements of the elite, then the destruction of the elite brings about darkness. If we ask instead about the lives of the great majority of people, the transition from slavery on great patrician estates to serfdom in feudal Christendom was a considerable improvement. Probably comparison of the lives of merchants, professionals, and artisans would also show improvement.

With respect to the high culture, there was certainly a major setback. Huge temples, palaces, and monuments could not be built without the concentrations of wealth that characterized the empire. In a time of political breakdown, cities suffered immensely. Viewed in these terms, a few centuries following the collapse of Rome can rightly be called "dark."

Even in that period, however, there was no lack of interest in "high culture." The monasteries did their best to preserve the results of classical learning. And as the feudal order took hold, architecture copying the classical reappeared and eventually developed into the more advanced and impressive Gothic. The medieval cathedrals were achievements of which the classical world was incapable. It is also striking that the artisans of the medieval world quickly developed new technologies in fields in which the classical world was static. The enormous achievements of modernity are rooted in the Middle Ages more than in the classical world that modernity has so admired.

Medieval education also far outran any achievements of antiquity. The medieval universities were unequaled in all the world. They survived into modern times despite the less congenial context, and provided the ideals for liberal arts colleges until the mid-twentieth century when finally modernity destroyed them. They were authentic centers of intellectual life, whereas the value-free research universities that have succeeded them discourage probing and creative thought. This extinction of intellectual activity in our educational system largely ended the great educational experiment of Christendom, but, of course, not totally. The Roman Catholic Church still continues in theory, and to a lesser extent in practice, some of its elements.

The Holy Roman Empire aimed to emulate the church in geographical extension, but it fell far behind. It certainly lacked any spiritual hold over those it ruled, for few people would find their identity in terms of this empire. And, as its name suggests, it did not threaten the overall self-understanding of Christendom. For centuries, "nations" did not disturb the remarkable unity of this Christian society.

Where was Abba in all this? Of course, if Abba was working intimately in the lives of believers in the early church, Abba was working in others as well, then and at all times. But the experience of that intimacy and lives derived from it were marginalized. For the great majority of people, the church provided a meaningful understanding of who they were and what they were to do. At its best it supported them in life's crises and reassured them that God was with them. But the church saw itself as mediating between them and God.

People were encouraged to pray. But their prayers were likely to be cries for help rather than intimate conversations laden with the expectation of loving guidance. God was still Father, but more often ruler and judge. Even Jesus took on these characteristics to such an extent that people *en masse* turned to Jesus' mother in hopes that she would be sympathetic and merciful. In Mary, to some extent God became again the Abba of Jesus. By making of her "the Mother of God" and "the Queen of Heaven," the medieval Mary could assume much of the role of Abba.

Mary was in fact the object of worship and devotion for many. In that sense she did become God and she had many features of Abba.

However, she could not herself be seen as "God" because the meaning of "God" was no longer shaped primarily by Jesus. The term *God* was reserved for an all-male Trinity that had evolved a long way from the experience and teaching of Jesus.

In the Middle Ages the greatest respect was directed toward the "saints." Whereas for Paul all Christians were saints, the church gradually distinguished saints from ordinary Christians. The saints provided the norm toward which all might strive. Those who seriously wished to achieve inner purification and sanctity in total devotion to God were encouraged to separate themselves from the world with vows of poverty and celibacy and to join monastic communities. There, people were more likely to seek intimacy with God, and no doubt this sometimes had the character of fellowship with Abba.

However, the spirituality of the monastery often moved more in a mystical direction. What was sought was sometimes not personal intimacy and mutual love, but the purification of the soul from all earthly attachments and from all that blocks unity with God. We associate medieval piety more with mysticism than with the sort of Spirit that Paul writes about in his communities.

The medieval figure who most fully renews Jesus' relation with Abba in a publicly visible way was St. Francis. As with Jesus, his loving fellowship with Abba was at the same time a deep love for all people and, indeed, all creatures. Like Jesus, his love extended to enemies. He bears witness that Abba was not absent in the church of Christendom.

Of course there were serious problems with this system. It fell far short of embodying the characteristics of the communities in which Jesus saw God's purposes already being realized. Once the church became powerful and wealthy, those who desired power and wealth were attracted to its leadership. Although greed and pride were identified as sins, they remained prominent. Medieval society may not have been as oppressive as most earlier societies, but it remained highly hierarchical in both its secular and its ecclesiastical dimensions.

3. Abba and the Creator, Lawgiver, Judge in Early Modernity

The most important factor in the erosion of Christendom was the renewal of nationalism. The world prior to the rise of Christianity was composed politically of ethnic groups and/or their control by an imperial power. Christendom depended on the primacy of Christian identity and a focus beyond ethnicity or political control. People understood themselves first and foremost as Christians, and secondarily in terms of a social role and locality. The shared language was Latin. The spoken languages were endlessly varied.

The elitism of the medieval world was heightened by the linguistic situation. Most people understood only a local language that had no written form. This limited their community of discourse to a small group. Even in that community, the most important shared activity, worship, was conducted in a language they did not understand—Latin, the only written language. Those who knew Latin were part of a vast cosmopolitan society, and this elite clearly had great advantages, which enabled them to exploit the illiterate majority.

For excellent reasons, an interest developed in making the scriptures, and other writings, available to people in their own languages, and committed scholars carried through the task of translation. No longer could the church authorities control the popular understanding of God. People could study the Bible for themselves, and among the results was the possibility of rediscovering

Abba. To some extent it was Luther's partial rediscovery of Abba that led to his break with Rome.

The unintended results of translating the Bible into Western European languages may have outweighed the intended ones. Luther had to create a national language. In any wide area of Europe, a great range of languages, most of them quite similar, were spoken. To develop a written language one local language or another had to be used, and as people learned to read the vernacular writings in this form, it became the shared language of a people. A common language supports a common culture and a common understanding of history. Nationalism, which had been a marginal phenomenon in the medieval period, revived.

National feeling supported the great split within the church caused by the Protestant Reformation. The wars that were exacerbated by this split were resolved by the agreement that princes would decide the religion of their people. This marked the end of Christendom. Of course, in Catholic Europe much of the medieval character of Christendom survived, but even there, nationalism grew strong. For many Europeans national loyalty soon trumped their religious identity or became entangled with it.

In the Middle Ages, kings and emperors were typically crowned by the church. This symbolized divine legitimization. The remaining power of theism in the early modern period prevented political rulers from simply asserting themselves as those with de facto power, and it certainly prevented them from claiming divinity as ancient rulers had done. Various strategies emerged to legitimate their rule. One was to claim "divine right" for kings. The American experiment was different: God's role was to endow individual human beings with rights that they could exercise to choose their own rulers.

The most secular approach was to derive the need of government from the state of nature, that is, the supposed situation when there was no government. The worse that situation was depicted, the more it could be assumed that individuals voluntarily surrendered their freedom to those who could enforce order. In this way, worldly power was legitimated without appeal to God, as long as it maintained the requisite law and order. The path to totalitarianism was prepared, and avowedly atheist governments have tended in that direction.

In this political debate about the legitimacy of national leaders, the issue of theism versus atheism was important, but the God being discussed had little to do with Abba. Where Abba functioned at all it was in private piety. However, the opponents of God pursued the remnants even there. This took place through the developments of which modernity is most proud, science and technology.

The technological developments of the medieval period encouraged increasing scientific experimentation. This was associated with various worldviews, Aristotelian, Platonic, and mechanistic. In the eighteenth century, the third won out. Modern science became identified with the search for the mechanisms that determine what happens, and it emphatically excluded any questions about purpose. Since God could not be part of the machine, his only remaining role was creating it and laying down the laws by which it functioned.

Within the churches, there continued to be intense discussions of deeply personal matters such as justification and sanctification, faith and works, justice and mercy, law and gospel. Abba played a role in this, and at the popular level, the eighteenth century was a time of great revivals of piety. As "Mary" had mediated some of the characteristics of Abba in the medieval world, "Jesus" and the "Holy Spirit" played this role in evangelical Protestant piety. John Wesley was the greatest of the evangelists and, in deeply personal ways, his preaching reintroduced both the teaching of Jesus and Paul's understanding of the transforming work of the Spirit.

In the increasingly secular world, on the other hand, discussions of God focused on just two points, morality and creation. God was viewed as ultimate moral judge. Since rewards and punishments are not justly distributed in this life, belief that they work out rightly after death played an important role in encouraging morality. God was also understood to be the original creator of all things and of the natural laws that govern them. This could be combined with the view that God occasionally set aside his own laws so that supernatural events occurred. But many saw no reason to believe this ever occurred. These are called deists, and in the eighteenth century, deism became the default position for the elite. Clearly Abba was not considered at all.

Until the middle of the nineteenth century, people assumed that they were not part of "nature." The medieval great chain of being had been replaced by a sharp dualism of human souls and the material world. This allowed people to accept the scientific, reductionist view of nature while attributing a large role to human reason and choices. Humanism was a natural part of modern thinking. Indeed, moderns claimed to be more humanistic than medieval thinkers because moderns attributed less to God.

4. Modern Atheism and the Resurrection of Abba

Charles Darwin threw a monkey wrench into the dualistic thinking that dominated the early modern period. The result has been that atheism has triumphed in Western culture. Obviously, that puts an end to serious consideration of Abba. My thesis is that another response to evolution is more reasonable, and that if it were adopted, it would open the door to a very serious consideration of Abba.

This book is proposing that today we are in a radically new position with respect to Abba. On the one hand, modern historical scholarship enables us to clarify Jesus' teaching about Abba and, on the other, developments in science show that just this kind of God fits the evidence. Chapter 1 focused on the first of these points. Chapter 2 has traced the history of thought about God through long periods in which Abba was marginalized, to a contemporary situation in which all the other ways of thinking of God have been marginalized. My thesis is that the door to seriously considering Abba has been opened.

In this section of the chapter, I will sketch how evolutionary thinking could open up the possibility of identifying Abba's role in nature after a period in which it had been systematically excluded. I recognize that the dominant community rejected this alternative. I will show that this rejection was not the result of evidence or argument, and that the victorious position is in fact quite weak. I will call for its overthrow.

When I dismiss the dominant thought-system in a few pages, the reader is likely to be skeptical. Accordingly, I devote a whole chapter to this topic for those who are interested. Chapter 4 summarizes the areas in which evidence against the dominant position is gathering strength. Obviously, the task of overthrowing the dominant contemporary worldview and its atheistic assumptions is not simple, but in my view the assumptions of this worldview are rather simple and, indeed, rather obviously mistaken. It is time to take note of the fact that the emperor has no clothes.

The great change between the early modern period and the one in which we live was the result of the evolutionary understanding of nature and including human beings in nature. This undercut the dualism that had dominated the earlier period. It also undercut the early modern idea that the complexity of the present world can only be explained by positing a divine Creator. Evolution shows how the present complexity arose by natural causes from a much simpler origin.

Since human beings emerged in a gradual process from a pre-human species, we are part of the same nature as the other animals. We may be distinctive, and the differences between the fully developed *Homo sapiens* and all other species may be very great. But the differences are not, as the early moderns thought, metaphysical.

If we are part of nature, then, it is common sense to think that nature cannot be merely objective, merely material, merely mechanistic. We humans know ourselves first and foremost in our subjectivity. We feel, we see, we plan, we hope. We suppose that the other animal species that are closest to us are likely to have subjective experiences somewhat like ours.

The result of these considerations was to renew something like the medieval great chain of being, now enriched with vastly increased biological information and much clearer ideas about how the more complex forms emerged. Much of the thoughtful public moved in this direction under the influence of Henri Bergson, William James, John Dewey, and many others. Some of us judge that the most comprehensive and thoroughgoing formulation of this alternative was that of the mathematical physicist, Alfred North Whitehead.

However, scientists in general resisted any change in their assumptions and methods, and their prestige in universities was decisive. The result was the extension to human beings of the assumptions and methods of the natural sciences. The deep-seated habit was to assume that scientific explanations were in principle comprehensive; so the objects of scientific study were taken to be the only real things. When human beings were included among the things to be studied, the same assumptions and the same methods were to be used. Scientism, defined by the metaphysics adopted by one group of scientists during the Renaissance, was victorious. Common sense was set aside.

The wide acceptance of the modern materialist worldview is based on the authority of science. Currently, that authority supports a worldview that is neither sensible nor supported by the findings of science. But when we understand the situation clearly we can freely reject this worldview. Fortunately, another worldview is available, one that is much more appropriate to our experience and to the scientific evidence. For my own part, this knowledge liberates me to shake free of contemporary orthodoxy.

Evolutionary thought allows us to suppose that God acts in the rest of nature somewhat as God acts in us. This action is always in experience. It does not force or compel us; instead it calls or lures us. There is much in the evolutionary process that suggests that in addition to the pushes from the past there is an effort in the present to make the most of whatever opportunities there are. Abba is at work.

3

Personal Experience of Abba

Chapter 4 will take up the apologetic task of developing the argument briefly indicated in the last part of chapter 2. However, before pursuing this apologetic task, we need to clarify what it is that Abba is doing in us and with us. I write here largely in a confessional style about how I understand Abba to work in my own life.

1. Sensing the Divine

Most people have some experiences that lead them to marvel. Music may arouse not only marvel but also other feelings that suggest the divine. It may arouse an unutterable longing or joy. Or it may evoke a deep feeling of peace and assurance.

A friend recently told me of how it felt to be on a mountain peak with beautiful vistas in all directions. Another may sometimes feel in a forest a communion with all the life there. Some may be brought to tears in hearing a story of heroism and self-sacrifice. Some find in the mass a depth of inexpressible meaning. For still others a long period of silent meditation may culminate in a sense of absolute presence. Sexual intercourse may occasionally lead to feelings of connectedness and fulfillment that go far beyond the pleasurable physical sensations.

In these and many other instances people realize that the world contains possibilities that cannot be measured in terms of degrees of pleasure, enjoyment, or satisfaction. There is something more, something much more, a treasure or many treasures that belong to a different dimension of experience. These moments of blessedness feel like a gift. It is natural to give thanks.

Some people also decide to pursue these experiences. Different forms of meditation can achieve some of them or at least make their occurrence more likely. Some can be approximated through the use of drugs. Repeated participation in rituals or repeated exposures of ourselves to the natural contexts in which these events occur is certainly possible. My own judgment is that the marvelous and special experience is rarely repeated in its fullness when it is sought in any of these ways, but much of value is still obtained.

In my own life, one special experience stands out. I was in the army during World War II, stationed in Washington, D.C. and renting a room in Arlington, Virginia. One night I knelt beside my bed to pray. Suddenly the room seemed filled by a spiritual presence that was totally accepting and loving. The joy and peace I felt was qualitatively different from any I have experienced before or since. The sense of a loving presence lasted only a few minutes, but the joyful memory remains.

I believe that special experiences like this are a very important part of life. I believe that God is involved in all of them. But this chapter is not primarily about them or even any subset of them that is especially likely to be called "religious." In setting these aside without denying their occurrence or diminishing their importance I am guided by the New Testament. Jesus does not talk about special experiences. He spent much time in prayer, and he may have had moments of ecstasy, but they were not his topic. He gave his disciples instructions on prayer, but the prayer in question was not about private religious experiences. He gave no instruction about spiritual disciplines that might lead to mind-alteration.

Paul referred to dramatic signs that sometimes accompanied his preaching and spoke positively of the ecstatic experiences that broke out in his congregations. But they were incidental to his central concerns. If special transnormal experiences are what is meant by the experience of God, then Jesus and Paul are remarkably indifferent to whether or not we experience God.

The Protestant Reformers can be read as even discouraging the quest for this kind of religious experience. For them, the right relation to God is one of faith. For them, faith meant primarily belief and trust. Belief and trust have profound effects on the rest of experience. So this is not to depreciate experience. But they do not directly involve transnormal experience of God. The quest for such experience is often described as mysticism, and the Reformers viewed this ambivalently.

The views of Jesus and Paul provide a third way between "religious" experience and divine absence. Jesus experienced Abba as fully present. On the cross there is a cry of abandonment that suggests that he lost that sense of God's presence, and that, indeed, this was his greatest suffering, but this was not his last word.

We get more light on *how* God is present in human experience from Paul. He had a strong sense of God's presence in the community as Holy Spirit, working internally in every believer. He could speak also of what God's grace is doing in the individuals and in the community. This working of the Holy Spirit is certainly experientially known or felt. Thus God is experienced. The experience of God in the New Testament is primarily the experience of grace, which is God's working in the hearts and minds, and even the bodies, of the faithful.

2. Divine Companionship

Calling God "Abba" is almost inseparable from experiencing God as present. Further, it suggests that the presence is supportive and interactive. It is the presence of a companion.

In my youth I experienced God as my companion. I did not spend much time in prayer, but I talked with God quite a lot. Of course, I did not hear a responding voice. A skeptic could say I was just talking to myself. But I experienced it as talking with God. With God I could be completely honest, because I felt that there was nothing hidden. But I felt that I was also completely understood and completely forgiven. Talking to myself in any such way would have felt silly.

I had my own "death-of-God" experience, and its deepest meaning for me was the loss of this companion. I felt alone as I had never felt before. Praying as before did indeed feel like talking to myself; it felt empty and foolish. I am glad to say that I have recovered some of my youthful sense of companionship, although not all.

This brief account makes clear that there is a close relationship between belief and experience. Understanding this relationship is fundamental to identifying and appraising the experience of God. One view is that beliefs are all-determinative, that when I believed that I experienced a divine companion, I interpreted my experience in that way and acted accordingly, and that when I ceased to believe that God exists, I could no longer organize my experience in that way. In this view, experience has no evidential force at all. We must decide on our beliefs independently of experience.

My account gives considerable support to this view. There is no doubt in my mind that experience is deeply shaped by beliefs. The philosophical empiricists who want to start with uninterpreted data inevitably fail. The data can only be the data of experience, and there is no experience that does not interpret its data. Of course, some layers of interpretation can be peeled away, and empiricists rightly encourage us to move in that direction in most circumstances. But what we then have is still interpreted.

This fact that all experience is interpreted or, perhaps more accurately, an interpretation, also accounts for the fact that existing features in the field of our experience sometimes cannot be experienced. Some people who are truly loved by others cannot experience that love. Their previous experience of rejection has shaped their experiential capacities. Many of us cannot remember certain past events. This inability to experience does not indicate that what we don't experience did not happen to us.

In every moment my experience contains innumerable data of which a very few are conscious. This selection is partly physical, but much of it is based on my currently dominant interests, needs, purposes, and dispositions. These lead me to see and highlight particular data and ignore others. The question is not whether selectivity is good or bad. It is inescapable. Two people walking side by side and surrounded by almost identical sounds, colors, and odors may have quite different sensory experiences even if both are being attentive to the data of their senses. The difference is increased if one of them is an absent-minded professor like me, whose immediate environment may be dominated by memories and theories rather than current sensory inputs.

Another example is sensitivity to the feelings of others. For one woman the most important data of experience consist in the anxieties, the joys, and the hesitations of those around her. A man sitting beside her may be almost oblivious to these while able subsequently to describe the actions of these people with great precision. Both the feelings and actions are real parts of the environment of both people. What we fail to experience is no evidence of its nonexistence, whereas the experience of something is some evidence of its existence.

I hope you will now see the relevance of this excursus to the question of whether the fact that my loss of belief in God's reality led to a loss of the experience of divine companionship is evidence that I in fact never experienced the divine. My view is that it is not, that my not experiencing divine companionship did not mean that God ceased to be there. To advance the discussion, I will describe my condition somewhat more fully.

I grew up in a home and a wider community in which belief in the sort of God who could be a companion was common. The most thoughtful and committed adults were also those for whom the relationship with God was most important. As a thoughtful child it is easy to see that I would assimilate this belief effortlessly. This thinking about God was accompanied by an emphasis on the internal lives of human beings, our motives and our feelings. You thought of yourself in this way, and were likely to be sensitive to the thoughts and feelings of others. I-thou relations were far more important than I-it relations.

This meant that what was most real and important for me was not what is given by the senses. To some extent it may be inferred from what is given by the senses, but the extent of that is debatable. The most natural expression of the experience is that there is a more direct relation between yourself and your feelings and other people and their feelings. Sensory observation is secondary. In that world, the fact that you have no sensory experience of God does not count against the strong feeling of God's reality and presence.

I learned in my late teens that this world in which I grew up was considered by intellectuals and scholars to be somewhat quaint. For some centuries the history of Western thought had replaced that world with another. In this other world, subjects, if they exist at all, play no causal role. Only objects can explain what happens. It was this profound shift in worldview that had led to the immense gains in science, of which I already stood in awe.

To cling to the world of subjects that had been my youthful world was to think and live in conflict with modernity with all its gains. I still assumed that there are people other than myself because there was sensory evidence of their existence, but there was no reason to give special attention to their motives and feelings. They, and myself, should be viewed primarily physically. Obviously no idea of God made any sense in this context.

This came to me as an enormous shock. The discovery that what had seemed to me to be thinking at the cutting edge was actually centuries out of date did not immediately change my thinking. I decided I needed to study modern thought before abandoning my youthful, Christian vision. I hoped I could comprehend the modern without giving into it completely.

However, some months of immersing myself in the literature of the modern world in a variety of fields left me in near despair. The modern understanding is so pervasive, so self-assured, and so consistently objectivist and reductive, that I assimilated these assumptions. Much of the literature that dealt with human experience dealt with it as it was already reshaped by this world. My death-of-God experience was one of defeat before the overwhelming impact of modernity.

Yes, a change of belief systems led me to cease to experience God as a companion. But no, that did not necessarily mean that my previous experience of God's companionship had no evidential value. It could mean that once my attention shifted from subjects to objects, whatever continuing presence of subjects there was in my experience faded, and the experience of a subject that could never be the datum of sense experience was obliterated.

In order to resolve my problem, I enrolled in the Divinity School of the University of Chicago. I found there a community of people who took nothing for granted but found that the dismissal of purpose, love, and meaning from the world was itself problematic. The dismissal was based on assumptions that should be questioned. The discussions in this different context helped me come to a better balance of subjects and objects, and gave me the ability to challenge the dominant form of the modern world in ways that did full justice to its legitimate claims. In this process, God gradually became real for me again, this time, more clearly than before, in the form of Jesus' Abba.

3. The Call Forward

The experience of God is not limited to companionship. We experience God especially in what I name "the call forward." I want to describe the feature of experience of which I am speaking in a way that you will recognize in your own experience as well. Instead of attending to the objects of sense experience, please focus on your experience as a whole, as it actually occurs, moment by moment.

We will agree with modern scientism that there is a lot of determination of the present by the past, and that much of our experience conforms to the mechanical model. Experience in one moment is very much like experience in the previous moment. This does not seem to be a choice; it is a given. The past experience impresses itself on the present. The repetitive aspect of experience is a product of a cause in a way that fits the general modern view.

Further, much of the change comes from other features of the past. In the present moment, the data of sight and hearing are different from the data in the previous moment. The new stimuli explain the change. This also fits the deterministic model, and there are other changes in the body, specifically in the brain, that cause differences.

Other differences are caused more indirectly. Perhaps a new sound triggers a memory that brings with it a feeling of regret, or a new element in the visual field evokes an expectation that causes anxiety. Many of the complex aspects of experience lend themselves to more or less satisfactory explanations that do not break out of the deterministic model.

But there are other features of experience that conflict with the model. A major example is the sense that we choose or decide. Common sense uses this explanation frequently. "I decided to stay home this morning." If a friend tells us this, we understand it to mean that she could have gone out but chose not to do so. If we are committed to the modern worldview, we will assume that this is not accurate. What in fact happened was the only real possibility. We will suppose that she may be telling the "truth" in the sense that she felt as though she decided, but in fact she did what the past determined her to do. In this case it also determined her to experience illusions and now to describe the situation in that way.

From the modern perspective, the sense that one is deciding what to do is only part of the total determination that constitutes the reality. It is less often recognized by moderns that their view of the situation in this modernist way is, in turn, also determined by past circumstances, and one's belief that it is "true" provides no evidence in its own favor. Indeed, the modern scientistic vision leads to concluding that there is no such thing as reason or thought, no distinction between truth and falsehood, and nothing that could be called "meaning." Most adherents of the modern worldview do not press consistency very far in this direction.

There is, of course, no empirical evidence for these conclusions. They follow from a rarely examined metaphysics. When we realize this, we may be comfortable taking experience itself seriously and thinking about matters with the use of common sense.

Our actual experience includes making decisions. That is, we cut off some real possibilities of thought and action, adopting others. That means that in the present we are agents rather than simply the products of the past. We are not responsible for all that we are. We *are* products of the past. But we are responsible for just how we maneuver within the parameters the past sets for us, and over time the choices we make play a large role in shaping our character.

This changes the picture dramatically from the modern scientistic one into which our education socializes us. If we pay attention to our actual experience, we are likely to conclude that much of what happens at any point in time is determined by the past. But at that point in time, we are also causal agents. We really make decisions.

Our legal system makes sense only with these nonmodern assumptions. To judge whether someone should be punished, we must decide that this person could have acted otherwise. Our scientistic education denies that this is possible, but our legal system depends on common sense. It is not a very radical proposal to suggest that we take common sense and phenomenological evidence seriously despite academia's objections.

But if we take seriously ideas that are declared by the dominant philosophy to be impossible, we should accept the responsibility to provide a philosophical explanation. This can at least proceed some distance without going far beyond common sense. We can begin by asserting that there is a difference between what may happen and what does happen. There are more possibilities than actualities. Some possibilities for the future are actualized; some are not.

This seems so evident to common sense, that we usually feel no need for further analysis. However, the denial of this possibility by the modern scientistic thinker alerts us that further analysis is in fact needed. The question is: How can there be a possibility that is not a necessity? Where does it exist? Of course, we can say that it exists in our imagination. But this leads to a further question: How can a past, from which these ideas were absent, cause them? But even if that could be answered, it would not suffice to explain decisions. Some of the decisions are between several courses of action, all of which could readily be actualized.

Although modern scientism dogmatically rejected *possibility* from the scene, most of those who reflect about it recognize that our actual lives, and even the actual course of worldly events, require that there be some realm of possibility or potentiality along with the realm of the actual. There are often multiple potentials relevant to actual situations. In the field of quantum theory, it seems that this role of potentiality applies even to the most elementary entities. In human experience, we routinely understand ourselves and others in this way. If we accept this, then we can understand our experience moment by moment as the product of the interaction between the actualities of the past and the relevant potentialities in the present.

If the potentialities acted deterministically, as do the actualities of the past, then we can explain novelty in the present without introducing decision. But our experience is that we choose. The options among which we choose are limited, but they are multiple. They offer themselves as possibilities, not necessities. It is the reality of multiple possibilities that requires decision but does not determine what that decision is.

This section is about the secular experience of Abba. I have spoken of our experience of a realm of potentiality. Is that Abba? No, at least not necessarily. Some philosophers are content to affirm the existence of such a realm, leaving its nature and location not further examined. We could say, without further explanation, that the reality of this realm can explain freedom and novelty, two very important features of our experience that have been excluded from reality by modern thought.

I myself prefer to press the question and ask how and where this realm exists. To me the most plausible answer is that it exists in something like a cosmic mind. But if no further feature of experience supported that explanation, the theory that potentiality is located in a cosmic mind would be nothing more than a plausible hypothesis.

However, the evidence provided by normal experience does go further. There are many choices that seem quite arbitrary or simply a matter of personal preference. But there are others that have a moral feel. I feel a desire to follow one course of action but an urge or call in another direction. For example, I have become addicted to Sudoku. Sometimes I work on a puzzle without making a significant decision to do so. I just come to the Sudoku in the paper and work on it. But at other times, I want to work on a puzzle but recognize that there are more important things that need to be done. Then I am aware of deciding. Sometimes I do the puzzle anyway, but sometimes I decide against it even against my continuing desire. I experience this decision in moral terms. I feel I "should" take care of more important needs. I may, or may not, do so.

My point is that, if the alternatives offered by the realm of potentiality are simply possibilities, the thought of Abba does not force itself upon me, but if alternatives are felt as ranked, with some being objectively better than others, they present themselves in a moral and personal way. The realm of possibilities does not seem to provide us indifferently with a collection of abstractions.

This kind of moral experience is more accurately described as the experience of a call. The call to do the more important task is not one determining force among others. The call requires a decision, but it does not determine what decision I will make. I may be more or less responsive to the call.

Many years ago I wrote a book (*God and the World*) in which I described our experience of "the call forward." I thought I was original in using that phrase. Years later I discovered that Martin Heidegger, in his analysis of human existence—which he named *Dasein*—spoke of *der Ruf nach vor.* The English translation is "the call forward." I gave up the claim to originality, but I was pleased to find support for my phenomenological analysis.

Of course, there was a difference. I moved from "the call forward" to the "One who calls." Heidegger was an atheist; so he moved from "*der Ruf nach vor*" to our "*Geworfenheit*"—our "thrownness." We simply find ourselves as we are. There is, for him, no explanation.

In Heidegger, as with so many moderns, there is no argument for atheism. It is simply the given starting point. Heidegger recognizes that God is not part of modern thought and accepts the implications. In a strictly phenomenological sense, I believe the atheistic explanation results from the a priori atheism rather than from phenomenological analysis. Or, we might say, Heidegger accurately describes the experience of the atheist who has no way of grounding the experience in an objective better and worse. The more natural understanding, when the one who is called is not pre-committed to reject it, is that there is One who calls.

Since, as an atheist, Heidegger cannot agree with most who feel called, that one action is in fact objectively better than another, the only norm he can generate is self-determination. That action is best that is most fully one's own, least affected by the views of others. This is "*eigentlichkeit*." The English translators have rendered it "authenticity." The German more clearly expresses its intensely self-oriented character. This may not be irrelevant to Heidegger's attraction to the Nazis.

I am not intending to criticize Heidegger. Not to have been an atheist would have excluded him from the dominant philosophical community. His brilliant phenomenological analysis pointed him to a relationship beyond the given world. To avoid following that route, he developed a further description of the existence of those who could not affirm such a relationship. Having done that, he had no possibility of any norm grounded beyond the self. He made a virtue of that necessity.

I assume he was entirely sincere in each move. But it is not the case, phenomenologically, that the experience of the call forward naturally leads to total self-affirmation. It leads more naturally to an I–Thou relation, a relation to Abba. My argument is that when we free ourselves from the atheism inherent in modern metaphysics, Abba appears in our experience, quite normally, whenever we feel called to serve our neighbors or open ourselves to new ideas.

Most moderns remain hesitant to recognize "the call forward" at all. They have been taught that this call and all experience of better and worse are the internalization of parental teaching or socialization into the community's values. There is plenty of that, and such internalization is a necessary part of cultural formation. It may be what some people mean by "conscience."

But this kind of "conscience" is not the call forward. Heidegger makes the difference clear. If conscience is the internalization of society's requirements, then the call forward must be contrasted to that. I personally would prefer to use "conscience" in a more inclusive way, but what Heidegger and I call the "call forward" is not the internalized teaching of parents or society.

4. Inspiration and Providence

Inspiration is a term that almost immediately suggests an inspirer, even a divine one. Of course, many who use the term today do not intend that, but this has not ended its frequent use. There is much that seems inspired, and that no other (acceptably modern) term describes.

Perhaps the most common use of "inspiration" is in the arts. Great art, almost by definition, is felt to be inspired. The term is used not only to honor its quality and originality but also because artists so often tell us that they have been inspired. They have the sense that something beyond themselves is at work in and through them. They yield themselves to that greater power. They feel that the result is more than they could envisage and implement by their own thought and skill.

This applies not only in the composition of music or a play but also in the production. The greatest pianists do not try fully to control their hands in a conscious way. They yield them to the music. Their emotions both form and are informed by the music.

I can attest to experiencing some of this from time to time in my writing. Sometimes I plan carefully and implement the plan laboriously. But sometimes the thought flows on its own; I learn what I think as the words appear on the page. I feel "inspired."

In any such statements, we need to be cautious. Often what feels inspired at the time turns out to need a lot of revision. Inspiration certainly does not mean infallibility. The word has been almost spoiled by the talk of the biblical authors being inspired in such a way that they made no errors. This is a kind of inspiration that few have ever claimed for their own work, and certainly the biblical authors made no such claims. But I feel sure that sometimes they felt, and were, inspired.

I judge that what happens in the experience of inspiration is an expansion of the call forward. If we open ourselves to the call forward and do not resist or question it for some period of time, what happens in and through us will be the realization of the best possibility available moment by moment. What is possible depends on our capacities and skills. The call forward is always for what is possible in that moment given the circumstances, but especially given who we are and what we are capable of doing. What is possible bears the stamp of our style and thought, but it uses those and adds to them what is relevant and possible at just that moment. The poetry of the inspired poet is that poet's poem. No one else could have written it. But it is that poet's work ordered and enriched by a wisdom greater than hers or his.

Other actions can be inspired also. If someone seeks help from another, and both are truly open, the help that comes may express a wisdom greater than theirs. An athlete may play as one inspired; a philosopher may have a surprising insight; a car driver, to avoid collision, may make moves that are beyond what he could have calculated in the moment; a speaker may respond to changing circumstances in a way that he could not have thought out in advance.

Sometimes in the morning, before beginning the day's work, I calculate carefully how to organize my time. At other times I relax, almost drowse, and suddenly I recall a task undone, a promise unfulfilled, or a good suggestion that I had forgotten. Sometimes I realize that I need to change something that I thought was complete. Sometimes what had been a jumble takes on a satisfying shape.

This is the working of the indwelling Spirit or the divine companion. Of course, those who deny that there can be any such thing will attribute these phenomena to the working of the brain, and surely they are not wrong. The brain is very much involved. But the inspiration seems to come from a source of novelty and wisdom that is hard to identify with a network of neurons. In a world not controlled by modern metaphysics, the interpretation of inspiration as the work of the Spirit would at least be considered alongside other explanations. It would often have the advantage of being supported by the self-understanding of the experience itself.

Thus far I have been speaking of the direct experience of Abba as being with me and as calling and inspiring me. Once we are open to seeing Abba's hands in the experiences of our individual lives, we can ask whether God's work sometimes shapes events for our good quite apart from our understanding or appreciation at the time.

Some have said that everything that happens is for the best. They suppose that even terrible earthquakes and wars express God's providential care for the world. They cite Romans 8:28, which, in the King James translation stated that "all things work together for good . . ." But the more accurate translation given in the Revised Standard Version tells us "in everything, God works for good . . ." Even in the midst of devastating events that do not express Abba's purposes, Abba works for good.

To claim that all things work for good is to invite incredulity and even anger from many people. I for one do not believe it. It implies that God willed the accidents in which children are killed, and also the global warming that now poses such a serious threat to our species. It would be distressing to me if Jesus taught that about Abba. So far as I can see, there is no evidence that he did so. I would be disappointed to find that Paul understood the Holy Spirit to cause wars and earthquakes. But so far as I can see, he taught nothing of the kind. Jesus and Paul both believed, and I believe, that in all things, whatever the situation, however bad it may be, however little good is possible within it, Abba works for good.

To believe in providence does not mean that God has a plan for each of us, which remains always unchanged. Quite the contrary. The changing situation requires new responses, and according to our responses in one situation, we develop new capacities or lose forever some opportunities for good. Nevertheless, God certainly knows what is possible as we do not, and sometimes closes doors that at the time seem promising so that we will find what are, in fact, the more fruitful paths.

In my old age, as I reminisce about my life, I am astonished at the extent that it now seems that things worked out better than they would have if there had been other moves, at the time more attractive. I will mention only one. When I completed my doctoral studies and sought a teaching position, there were very few jobs available and lots of competition for those. I had entered school after separation from the army at the same time that many other veterans were benefiting from the government program to enable us to get an education. Colleges were expanding and scraping the barrel to have enough teachers to meet the great demand. I completed my program at just the time that the number of veterans going to school was declining and the number of new PhDs increasing. I was lucky to get a job at a little junior college in Appalachia teaching whatever no one else was available to teach.

The dean of the University of Chicago Divinity School, where I had just finished my doctoral studies, wanted to bring me back to teach there. Professionally there was no comparison between the position he wanted me to take and the one I had. If the job had been offered me I would have considered my dreams fulfilled. However, at that time the Divinity School was part of the Federated Faculty. Appointments required the agreement of the heads of all the schools. One of them vetoed my appointment. That door was shut. I continued teaching introductory courses in various fields to junior college students.

At the time, this was keenly disappointing. But looking back, I'm glad that I was denied the position at Chicago. I realize that the opportunities that actually developed in my life, while never matching Chicago in prestige or salary, enabled me to do things that

I could never have done there, things that now seem more important in the larger scheme of things and, at any rate, far more satisfying.

I am enough of a "modern" myself that I often say I am lucky that my going back to Chicago to teach was blocked. Luck is the secular interpretation, and I believe that much of what happens is rightly attributed to chance. Jesus thought so too. He criticized those who supposed that people who had been crushed in an accident must have deserved their fate in some way. For him, it was just chance. But when I survey my life, I see a half dozen other turns it could have taken that looked good at the time but would not have afforded the opportunities I finally had. The appeal only to luck seems forced.

I do not want to bore you with the details of my career, but I will give an important example of what I mean. Late in life, to my utter surprise, by what seem strange coincidences and chance, I became a person with some influence in China and some ideas of how to use that influence. I think I have contributed a little to a shift of Chinese government policy away from industrializing agriculture to trying to save the rural villages—to develop them instead of bulldozing them. I believe this is important for hundreds of millions of Chinese and for China's responses to social and environmental crises in the years ahead. There are still great pressures toward industrializing agriculture. The outcome is far from settled. My influence is a minor factor. But at least it has contributed to making the future of rural China a topic of discussion in high places.

As a Christian theologian it had never occurred to me to prepare for such a role in an atheist nation. Yet the opportunity presented itself, and I was prepared. As I consider all the special circumstances that led to that outcome, it is hard for me to avoid thinking that Abba's hands were in these events. This sense of providence is heightened when I consider all the special developments in the lives of other key people whose roles have been more important than mine.

In a world in which so many terrible things happen, it is very dangerous to talk of providence at all. If God could bring something positive at one point, we ask quite reasonably, why did God not prevent this or that horror or make some other good thing happen. My guess is that God often fails. We are not puppets. I like to think I was responsive from time to time, even though I know that I would have made different choices at many points if I could have. No matter my availability and willingness, if one or two other people had not made surprising and remarkable decisions, nothing would have happened. Humans often derail God's plans. And some of the things people wish God had prevented may not have been preventable at all. My affirmation that special providence is real in no way implies that God always succeeds. But my experience leads me to thank God for shaping my career beyond my understanding. Those who believe it's all the luck of the draw are welcome to their interpretation. I have been forced by experience to give it up.

5. Healing

Although Jesus' primary concern was to make the presence of the divine commonwealth known and to lure people into the life that it offered, much of his time was spent in responding to immediate human need. In most cases this was for healing, and still today, when people ask for prayers, it is most often for healing. In those days there were professional doctors, but there were also faith healers. According to the gospels, and I see no reason to be skeptical, Jesus was extraordinarily effective in this role.

The Protestant churches that were mainstream a generation or two ago, encourage prayer for the sick, but they assume that professional care of medical doctors and psychiatrists now supersedes faith healing. Still, at the margins of these churches and more prominently in others, faith healing has continued to flourish. Although its successes are sometimes exaggerated, and some of the supposed successes may have been staged for TV audiences, authentic faith healings, some quite remarkable, continue to occur. Charismatic people can engender medically unexplained healings today, just as in Jesus' time. Western faith healers have been joined by Eastern practitioners, often with quite different methods and less attention to "faith." We may be skeptical of particular stories in our gospel accounts, but it would be wrong to discount the role of healing in Jesus' brief ministry. Certainly he healed, and clearly he understood that in doing so he was working with God. Jesus' Abba is a healer.

In considering the healing effects of Abba's presence in human experience, I do not want to focus on the extraordinary instances of which the gospels are full. They are worthy of study, but in this book I am chiefly interested in the ordinary, everyday working of God in our lives and in the world. There is much to marvel at in the common world of our ordinary experience. If we find God there, we can see God also in the extraordinary. If we focus on the extraordinary, we may miss God's presence in our day-to-day experience.

I am repeatedly surprised by how rapidly wounds heal when the body is given the chance. Doctors often comment that their medicines do not heal us. They counter hostile forces in the body. When these are removed, nature works its healing power. When thought and emotions are healthy and supportive, the healing work of nature is speeded and strengthened.

For me, there is no "nature" from which Abba is absent. That does not identify God and nature. There is much in nature other than Abba. But I think that it is Abba's presence in nature that makes for healing. I believe that Abba is in every cell in the body calling it to do its part for its own well-being and for the well-being of the whole.

When we pray for healing for ourselves, we are aligning ourselves with Abba's working within us. We are also directly affecting our bodies, encouraging the cells to be open to what Abba wants to do in them and with them. When we pray for healing for another person, what is happening? Are we expressing an idle wish? Are we hoping to change Abba from indifference to concern? Are we exerting telepathic power on the one for whom we pray so that in fact the form of "prayer" is irrelevant? Or are we working with God in the healing process? I like to think it is this last. How can we imagine that this works?

Let us suppose that Abba is in all things calling them to achieve what they can for themselves and for the wider good. In us, many factors enter into determining how effective Abba's work is, and Abba is working in all these events as Abba works in us. Many factors affect the effectiveness of Abba's work.

Let us suppose that the factors that affect the outcome of Abba's efforts include, but are not limited to, the physical situation. Operations and chemistry play a large role. But we also know that the patient's spirit has a large part to play. Let us, for the moment, assume that the patient's spirit is affected by the spirit of other people including some who are not physically present. There may be some influence all the time, but directed prayer may strengthen that effect. It may help to align the patient's purposes with those of Abba.

My speculations go further. There are many experiments that show that human emotion can affect the condition of cells without physical contact. The most effective relations are between you and the cells that make up your body. Next come your relations to cells in your immediate environment. Healing is often facilitated by touch. But distance does not necessarily change matters altogether. Our prayers may help the cells to follow Abba's call more fully. There is now evidence that even at the molecular level our emotions affect other entities in our environment.

In sum, with regard to all that I have said thus far, I believe that we experience in some usually faint and fragmentary way Abba's presence with us, working in all things for good. Abba's work is most effective if we attend to it, open ourselves to it, align ourselves with it. This is part of the meaning of faith. Our resulting thoughts and actions sometimes have effects beyond our intentions. We can experience ourselves to be participating in Abba's salvific work in the world. And we can sense the companionship of Abba as well as of others who work with Abba. We can know something of the divine commonwealth, the presence of which Jesus announced.

6. Truth and Reality

I conclude this chapter with a discussion that seems important to me, but may be too "philosophical" for ready appreciation. If readers already feel stretched to understand how Abba is intimately involved in their lives as companion, One who calls and inspires, a providential guide and healer, pass on to the next chapter. But for me it is also important that my sense of a real world and of real truths about it is bound up with my experience of, and belief in, Abba. So I cannot resist an effort to explain how this is so.

Many people are surprised to learn that the modern worldview, to which they are likely to be at least partially committed, consciously or unconsciously, denies that there is any reality prior to and independent of our experience. As a result, it undercuts the commonsense idea of truth. This is a result of the philosophical assumptions with which the modern mind is bound up. Modern thought profoundly conflicts with common sense. The reasons that moderns favor atheism and deny the objective reality of the world are intimately interrelated. These connections lie on the surface of modern philosophy. I have found understanding this truly liberating.

Common sense supposes that some statements correspond to reality and others do not. If I say that my son came to see me yesterday, common sense assumes that either it is true that he came to see me yesterday or it is false, because the reality of what happened yesterday is a given. Common sense assumes what is now labeled "the correspondence theory of truth." If what happened yesterday is not a given, then no present belief can either correspond to it or not correspond with it—"truth" and "falsehood" have to be redefined. The need for such a redefinition is the largely unquestioned outcome of modern philosophy.

When our acceptance of the implications of the modern worldview drives us to give up "the correspondence theory of truth," the most common alternative is "the coherence theory." If we do not ask about facts, but rather about belief, then this shift makes sense. I believe my son came to see me yesterday because I remember it. But someone may challenge the accuracy of my memory. Perhaps he came the day before. If this questioning shakes my confidence, I try to fit this memory with other memories and other forms of evidence. If it turns out that his having come the day before fits other bits of evidence better, I'll acknowledge that my memory is faulty. I'll accept as truth what coheres better with other parts of my belief system.

However, whereas common sense tells me that checking the coherence of alternative beliefs with other beliefs is a means of determining which belief corresponds with reality, the modern thinker asserts that the coherence itself provides the only valid meaning of "truth." My concluding that my son came to see me the day before yesterday is equivalent to saying "the belief that my son came to see me the day before yesterday" is coherent with my other beliefs. It is not a statement about my son or about past events. For those who accept modern metaphysics, the statement can only be about my current beliefs.

This shift away from commonsense realism is closely related with the rejection of God. Philosophers know this, and other academic disciplines rarely dispute it. However, since philosophy is now viewed as just one discipline alongside others, and one of questionable importance, this theoretical commitment is hardly conscious and, in practice (and I might add, fortunately) common sense often intrudes. The consistent implications of the modern worldview are not believable, but they still work to exclude God and much else.

My argument in this section is that we do experience truth as correspondence and even those who deny it still live as if they believed it. My argument further is that the experience of truth is inseparable from the experience of Abba. If we free ourselves from those modern assumptions that drive modern thought into positions that contradict what at a deep level we all know to be true, we can also recognize how deeply the God we know as Abba is present in our most ordinary experience. Let me explain.

A fundamental assumption of modern thought is that our experience relates us to the external world only through the senses. Actually, eyes are the sense organ that plays the overwhelmingly dominant role in modern thought. The Father of Modern Philosophy, René Descartes, took this for granted.

Descartes undertook to doubt everything he could doubt, so that he could rebuild philosophy on indubitable grounds. He could not doubt his own existence or that he was having visual experience. His vision gave him directly only patterns of color, that is, appearances or phenomena, but he *knew* that these were the colors of actually existing objects. This implied that we are constituted in such a way as to believe this. He considered the possibility that we are thus constituted by One who wants us to be deceived, but he held instead that we can prove by reason that the One who constitutes us is good and therefore not a deceiver. He clinched this account with the "ontological argument" for God, that is, an argument from the *idea* of a Perfect Being to the *actuality* of such a being.

Descartes, in this way, achieved a metaphysical dualism. For him, there is a real material world, and there is a real world of human souls that are not material at all. Clearly the Father of Modern Philosophy did not reject either belief in an actual world or the assumption that truth and falsehood refer to correspondence, or lack of correspondence, with that world. But he was clear that he could maintain this connection with common sense only by appealing to God.

Subsequent philosophers were uncomfortable with this appeal to God, and they developed their philosophies without it. David Hume expounded the implications of this effort most thoroughly and decisively. He accepted the fact that vision gives us only appearances or phenomena, and he worked out the consistent implications. These, clearly, include atheism. But they also include the loss of a real world. Without a real world, human beliefs cannot correspond with reality.

By that time the most important question for philosophers was the implications of their conclusions for the natural sciences. Hume's implications seemed disastrous. Science was the study of efficient causes. In the world Hume described, there can be no efficient causes. The only describable entities are appearances or phenomena, and these cannot exercise causality.

Immanuel Kant came to the rescue. He did not challenge Hume's analysis. But he posited that the structure of the human mind is such that we can only interpret phenomena in the way science did. In this way, "causality" was rescued, and scientists were encouraged to continue what they were doing. But the world was reduced to appearances.

Note the change from Descartes. Descartes assumed that we necessarily interpret sense data, the world of appearance, as derived from an actual world. For him it was important that we believe in the reality of this world. God was required in order to move from the world of appearance to confident affirmation of the actual world behind it. For Kant, it is enough to describe the structure of the mind as determining that we locate the appearances in spatial, temporal, and causal relationships. One does not ask whether they really have these relationships. So the question of God does not arise in this discussion. By giving up concern for a reality behind appearances, Kant could remove God from this discussion. Obviously, the correspondence theory of truth is irrelevant if there is no reality to which statements might correspond. Kant's overriding concern was to encourage scientists to continue doing what was proving so successful.

I should note that Kant himself was a theist. But since he accepted the modern view that our knowledge of the world is entirely dependent on sense experience, he excluded God altogether from "knowledge." He saw that this also excluded not only questions of correspondence with reality but also questions of morality and value.

He did not leave matters thus. For him, it was clear that human affairs cannot and should not be conducted according to the understanding of knowledge properly at work in science. The world of actual human life was extremely important. He distinguished the "practical reason," operative in the world of human affairs, from the kind of reason needed in science. In the world of practice, belief in God was needed and justified. Descartes's metaphysical dualism gave way to Kant's epistemological dualism; there is the world of theoretical knowledge, and there is the world of practice.

Kant has been by far the most influential thinker of the past two centuries. There are, of course, some philosophers who still hark back before Descartes for their grounding. The Roman Catholic Church maintains the tradition of St. Thomas Aquinas. This is realistic about the world, affirms truth, and, of course supports belief in God. On the other hand, the philosophies considered "modern" generally limit themselves to a phenomenal world. If they allow for God, it is a "God" who plays no causal role in the world. Either, as Kant taught, "God" is a "postulate" of practical reason, or "God" is the metaphysical ultimate irrelevant to the world of science and history.

Of course, very few people really live as if they believed what the modern worldview implies. When I was a student at Chicago a famous positivist philosopher was on the faculty, Rudolf Carnap. I attended his class, and he developed the implications of modern thought with beautiful rigor and consistency. When he was asked whether, when he went home, he lived according to those views, he said, of course not; his beliefs and his practice were entirely unrelated.

Those who are not able to divorce belief and practice to this extent have developed many alternatives that have popular following. These include writers like Martin Buber and Emanuel Levinas, who emphasize personal relationships in ways that ignore the limitations imposed by the modern worldview. Similarly many forms of therapy are deeply humanistic and some emphasize the importance of relationships. Asian nondual ways of thought have their following.

I am not saying that the modern worldview has swept everything before it. I am only saying that it dominates education, especially higher education, and thereby shapes what is regarded as expertise in most fields. Among modern scholars, nonmodern ideas are typically viewed condescendingly, and God's systematic exclusion is accepted even by many who make exceptions for human purposes and relationships.

The situation is particularly difficult for liberal Protestants. Protestantism arose as part of the modern rejection of medieval thought and culture. It was closely associated with emerging individualism and nationalism. In its more liberal form it wanted to be aligned with the best in modern thinking, and it thought that science was central to that. It supported and spread education, and although for a long period that was especially characterized by the liberal arts inherited from the Middle Ages, it continued its support when the modernist disciplines took over. In this way it came to support an educational system fundamentally committed to value-free atheism. Liberal Protestants often seem surprised when the children they have raised in the church turn their backs on Christian faith as they advance through the educational system.

The situation may change when we understand *why* God is excluded and the price paid by those who work out the consistent consequences of the doctrines that lead to this exclusion. The modern doctrines stand in sharp contradiction to common sense. If there are alternatives that allow us to take our own experience seriously, we should surely feel free to consider them.

Let's begin with the world as we actually experience it instead of as the modern worldview describes it. We experience our friends and family as individual human beings with their own subjective reality. It is that reality that first and foremost makes itself felt in our experience.

For example, I feel my friend's suffering or anger. I am told by those faithful to modern philosophy, that I imagine the anger based on visual and auditory cues. Of course, that can happen. If I am watching a movie, I do project feelings on images. But in normal human relations, especially those of great intensity, it does not feel like I am projecting feelings. I feel the other's feelings. Sometimes, indeed, I may be emotionally overwhelmed by the anger directed at me by another person.

This means that we live in a world of subjects. These subjects extend to other animals as well. Few of us doubt that our pets also see, hear, hope, and fear in ways not unlike our own. Common sense seems to extend this recognition of subjectivity more widely.

In short, modern philosophy is wrong in assuming that any conceptualizing of how we are related to others must begin with sense data. We know ourselves to be embodied because bodily feelings inform our experience. We know we have a past, because past experiences inform our current experience. We know we live in a social world because the presence of others informs our experience. Certainly the data of sight and hearing inform our present experience, but there is no phenomenological justification for giving them primacy.

Associated with the primacy of vision has been an understanding of the self as a substance, something that exists in itself and by itself. The Cartesian "ego" or "I" is imaged as an entity whose existence is prior to any particular experience. Buddhists pointed out long ago that there is no such substance. Every moment of experience is an event of "dependent co-origination." Whitehead describes it as "the many become one and are increased by one." The individual experiences are the ultimate actualities. The "I" is an abstraction from them, a very important abstraction. The experience of patches of color is also abstracted from these actualities—another important abstraction.

For modern thought, an actual world and true statements about it cannot be affirmed apart from *Deus ex machina*—God acting on the machine from without. Although this kind of God survived in the imagination for some time, it is obviously unattractive and has very little connection with the God of Abraham or Moses. It is totally alien to Jesus' Abba.

If we understand ourselves as syntheses of what has been, we do not need God in order to explain our profound sense of relatedness. We are syntheses of relations to others. Our knowledge of that is not inferred from something else. I started out to show how the experience of truth involves an intimate relation to God. Now I have shown that a deeper analysis of experience makes God dispensable in this regard!

What this means is that once we have rejected the idea that our knowledge of one another and of the past is derived from sense experience, we can recover a realistic view of the world. This same move removes the major reason for atheism, that is, that there is no path from sense experience to God. Once we recognize that our experience gives us direct access to past and present reality, we know that we do know some truths about the world. Since we can now take belief in God seriously, we can ask what role our experience of God plays in relation to our quest for truth.

I want to show that no *Deus ex machina* is relevant. My memory of my son's visit, even its confusion about dates, is all quite understandable without introducing God into the picture. My visit with him is still participating in constituting my present experience. I have immediate access to that past event. I can confidently hold to true statements about the conversations we had.

But my belief about the past extends far beyond those few events that still live vividly in my present experience. I believe that what happened in the past actually happened then. I believe there were patterns of relations among the events unknown to any of them, but nevertheless real. I believe that current statements about what happened either correspond or fail to correspond to the reality of what happened. For me to be correct, there must be a unified experience of the world that has to the past a relationship something like my most vivid memories. My deep confidence that there is truth about the past to which our research draws us more closely—that we are discovering what is there to be found rather than inventing it—is grounded, consciously or not, in my experience of Abba. Abba is Truth. And apart from Abba there can be no truth about most of the past.

In concluding this section, let's move from what may seem rather impersonal to the very intimate relation to Abba as Truth. Consider your experience in every moment. Often it contains emotions of which you are not aware. I have been told that I was angry and denied it, only to realize later that I had indeed been angry.

We know that we do not fully know ourselves. We go to psychiatrists to get help in understanding ourselves more fully. This implies that what we really are is not an inference from sense experience but a mysterious actuality. What I really am is what Abba knows me to be. One major form of spiritual practice is to seek, in relation to Abba, a deeper awareness and acceptance of ourselves.

4

Can Science Get Along with Abba?

In this chapter, I am returning to a topic treated both in the preface and in chapter 2. In those places I dealt with it glancingly to indicate how and why I felt free to believe much that modernity denies. I have proceeded to make many statements, especially about human experience, that modernity excludes a priori.

Now I want to justify my rejection of the modern worldview much more fully. Here I will treat it more rigorously and take the debate to the home ground of my opponent, that is, science. I am now directly challenging the exclusion of God from the modern university and the culture it expresses and transmits. I begin with a somewhat fuller account of how the exclusion came about.

I have also indicated that the exclusion of God is included in the exclusion of subjects from any causal role. My strategy in counterattacking modernity is to take up, first, the question of the role of subjects. Only if we recognize that common sense is correct in attributing agency to subjects, beginning with ourselves, is there an opening for discussing whether one of the subjects is divine and what role the divine subject plays.

1. Excluding Subjects from Higher Education

By the seventeenth century, Europe was keenly interested in deepening its knowledge of nature. This led both to philosophical speculation and empirical study. Some scientists were particularly interested in magnetism and focused on how natural objects attract and repel one another. Gravity remains a mystery for science even today. Some were engaged in analyzing complex entities into their parts, aiming to transmute one element into another. Their program did not pay off until the chemical revolution in the nineteenth century. Others focused on mechanics, growing directly out of the technological successes of the medieval period. This approach proved more immediately productive than the others, and thereby gained prestige.

The Aristotelian philosophy that largely shaped the late medieval mentality made a clear distinction between living things and inanimate objects. The Aristotelians studied the human body, for example, to understand the distinctive function of the different organs. When they understood the role of the heart in pumping blood through the body and traced the circulatory system, they were satisfied that they had gained important knowledge of nature.

The scientists who were impressed by the potential of the mechanistic approach, however, wanted to understand *how* the heart pumped blood. And to understand "how" was to show the mechanism. As they showed the mechanisms involved in living processes, they believed that they were showing that all of nature could be explained on the same principles as a clock, that is, as a system of pushes and pulls.

The argument of the mechanists against the Aristotelians could be put in terms of Aristotle's four causes: the formal, the material, the efficient, and the final. The Aristotelians thought that all four were important types of explanation, but in dealing with living things, they often focused on the final. That is, they believed that every part of the living body had a function in the whole, and that its structure could largely be explained by its role. The new mechanists thought that this emphasis on final causes kept one at a superficial level. They believed that everything happened as it did in obedience to laws about efficient causes. Until we understand how these operate in each case, we have no real understanding of why things are as they are and act as they do.

A world composed of things that are explained functionally suggests purposes. A house has the shape that it has because people wanted certain things in their home. Animals have hearts because hearts are needed for life. This suggests that "someone" aimed to bring life into being. The world expresses purposes, creaturely and divine.

A world of things that are explained mechanically suggests a deterministic system of cause and effect that could not be other than it is. Everything happens as it does because of the forces that impinge upon it. If it satisfies some purpose, it does so either by chance or by necessity, not because of the purpose.

In the seventeenth and eighteenth centuries, there was no intention to deny that human purposes play a role. The human world and its creation of artifacts were exempt from the mechanical world of nature whose secrets were being uncovered so successfully by the new science.

Most of the early moderns agreed that this enormously complex machine required a Creator and that the laws they discovered required a Lawgiver. They identified the Creator and Lawgiver as God. Some believed that the Creator and Lawgiver could also suspend the laws and make things happen that did not follow from natural causes. Many of them held this view in support of Christian doctrines about incarnation and resurrection and the belief that miracles continue to occur.

Others were convinced that once the world was created and the laws established, the Creator and Lawgiver took no further action. They considered the idea that some events are supernatural to be naïve credulity. Some might remain Christian, but they freed Christianity from the taint of superstition. Others rejected Christianity as irrational. They were often called Deists. Many of them retained the belief that after death people would be judged according to their obedience to the moral law. Their role was somewhat like that of those today who say they are "spiritual" but not "religious."

The dominant culture had no place for an Abba-like deity, but at the popular level there were occasional revivals of Christian piety, often deeply immersed in the Bible. Thinkers arising out of this piety played some role in later theological articulations. The most important was Friedrich Schleiermacher, who called himself a "pietist of a higher order." His theology was based on the human feeling of God. In his express account of this feeling, "God" was far from Abba, but his affirmation of the importance of feeling kept alive the possibility that feelings of Abba could play a role.

John Wesley in England led the most important revival of personal piety. His preaching stayed close to the biblical texts including the Sermon on the Mount, and so reflected the experience of Abba quite extensively. Thus Abba did not disappear from the eighteenth century, but the determinative course of intellectual life ignored the piety and thinking that related to Abba. And the pietists did little to challenge the mechanistic metaphysics that excluded subjectivity from playing any role in the nature science studied.

The crucial test came with Darwin's demonstration that human beings are part of nature. In popular discussion today, attention is focused on the arguments of conservative Christians against the acceptance of Darwin. Many wanted to reaffirm a special creation of human beings despite the evidence. Others wanted to show that evolution required divine intervention from time to time. These arguments continue. Attention to them, however, distracts from the more important debate. Emphasizing the conservative attack on the theory of evolution as a whole serves more to gain sympathy for the standard scientific view, than to give attention to real scientific alternatives, which, partly as a result of the prominence of the wrong debate, are now rarely considered.

Thoughtful people who did not get involved with the opponents of Darwin were left with two choices. Either they must understand themselves as part of the mechanical world in which their subjectivity ultimately played no causal role, or they must affirm that nature is more complex than had previously been allowed. Those who adopted the second option assumed that human feelings and purposes are important contributors to what happens in nature, and if humans are kin to other species, the feelings and purposes of other animals should also be recognized as contributing to the course of events.

Toward the end of the nineteenth century and in the first half of the twentieth, those who adopted this second view played an important role in cultural and intellectual circles. My involvement came during the last days of its importance. I will describe it, so that the reader will understand my distress at what happened and my commitment to change it.

I was in the U.S. army during World War II, and the GI bill enabled me to go to the University of Chicago after I was separated. After a year in the Humanities Division, I entered the Divinity School. My professors all belonged to the segment of the culture that thought it was important to rethink nature in view of our inclusion in it. They called this view "neo-naturalism." The Divinity School had been committed to neo-naturalism since the thirties, even though they focused more on the socio-historical method and the social gospel. In earlier decades Chicago was recognized as a leader in progressive theology, but by the time I was there, Chicago had been marginalized.

This change was due to the dominance of neo-orthodoxy. German liberal Protestantism had accommodated itself to German culture, and when this was taken over by the Nazis it offered little resistance. Significant resistance came only from a new biblicism that confronted the Nazis with a countercultural message from the Bible. Americans were learning that American liberal Protestantism was similarly acculturated and that serious Christians needed to ground themselves in the Bible and in classical Christian thought. Neither the socio-historical school nor neo-naturalism appealed to those who were excited about the new orthodoxy.

Nevertheless, the faculty of the University of Chicago Divinity School had sufficient self-confidence to continue on its way. The professors believed that it was a time of a ferment of ideas and that the task of the faculty was to encourage students to find their own way. Although they were all neo-naturalists, they did not impose the new naturalism on their students. Students were required to make a case for the position they adopted, whatever that might be.

Meanwhile in the wider context, the advocates of a new naturalism were being marginalized in a different way. This was not done by direct argument against neo-naturalist ideas. It took place by changing the subject. Many professors were convinced that arguing about philosophy was not an appropriate role for universities. Their job was to advance research on specialized topics. The physical sciences were viewed as providing the best models for research; so their methods were imitated in the social sciences and even in the humanities.

Robert Maynard Hutchins, the chancellor of the University of Chicago, was the last major educational leader in the United States to oppose the new understanding of what a university should be. I did not realize this when I was there as a student, but Hutchins was losing the battle, and not long after I left Chicago, he gave up the struggle.

Modern universities grew out of medieval ones. These were grounded in the liberal arts derived from the Greeks but given a Christian flavor. The liberal arts were supplemented by professional education. In the United States this model was adopted both in stand-alone liberal arts colleges and others where the college was supplemented by professional schools.

It is interesting that it took a long time for universities of this sort to fully integrate the natural sciences into their programs. In the early modern world, most natural-scientific research was independent of universities. In Germany, however, the view that some universities should specialize in research took hold. In the early nineteenth century, the University of Berlin was founded to do this.

Berlin gained great prestige, and other universities modeled themselves on it. More and more specialized areas for research were identified and guilds were formed to support scholars in research on these topics. The research university was organized in terms of these *Wissenschaften* or academic disciplines, and universities competed in the production of research.

The contrast between universities organized for research and those that prized the liberal arts is clear. The latter are focused on the general well-being of the students and their ability and motivation to serve the larger society. The former seek to advance knowledge at the frontier of research. The latter encourage original thinking about human well-being; the former teach how to do specialized research. The latter seek wisdom; the former aim to increase information.

The liberal arts colleges were natural contexts for discussing new ideas about nature and how human beings fit into it. But this is not a topic of any academic discipline. The disciplines adopt the Cartesian model of pure objectivity. They have no place to consider how subjective experience could play a role in determining what happens.

Robert Maynard Hutchins favored the intellectual ideal of the university as a place that encouraged free thinking and rigorous argument. But the broader academic community had accepted the organization of knowledge into academic disciplines designed to promote research on specialized topics. Hutchins was not able to stem the tide. The Divinity School lost its distinctiveness and ceased to be a center of neo-naturalist thought. The model of specialized research swept the university world. Since professors for liberal arts colleges were prepared in these universities, even what are still called liberal arts colleges have tended to become disciplinary in their curricula. Introductions to multiple disciplines, all of which favor value-free research, are not liberal arts.

Of course, not all higher education is now done in the value-free research mode. Much of it is designed to help students get jobs. Here and there elements of the liberal arts survive. A few colleges and universities experiment with quite radical models. But reflection on broad topics such as nature does not fit into the new system, which, with little reflection, assumed the Cartesian view of nature; so neo-naturalism has been pushed to the margins of higher education.

Some of us continue to believe that nature cannot be as described by Descartes in the seventeenth century. We remain convinced by the writings of such late-nineteenth and early-twentieth-century thinkers as Henri Bergson, William James, Charles Sanders Peirce, and Alfred North Whitehead. We believe that even the sciences that cling most closely to the seventeenth-century orthodoxy are providing evidence against their own model.

2. A World of Events, Not Objects

The greatest blow to the seventeenth-century metaphysics, which still dominates our research universities, came with the splitting of the atom. The word *atom* means what cannot be divided; so it is ironic that the name sticks to what was thought to be the atom in the eighteenth century. The term should have been shifted to electrons and protons, or quanta and quarks. One hesitation, I suspect, is that physicists are now aware of how difficult it is to know what cannot be divided. At a certain level, the meaning of "divided" itself becomes unclear.

The metaphysical problem, of course, is not that scientists made a mistake about the indivisibility of atoms. If it had turned out that the constituents of atoms could be viewed as still tinier material particles, the metaphysics would not be affected. But we all know that this is not the case. The quantum world is not much like the Cartesian one. It is more like a world of living subjects than a world of inanimate objects, but it is different from both.

Scientists have largely given up understanding the quanta on the basis of their views of objects. There is talk of trying to understand the world of objects in terms of what has been learned of the quantum world, but progress is very slow. If scientists could recognize that the world of objects has never existed except as an abstraction, the prospects would be much better.

One step in the right direction would be to give up the lingering substantialism that shapes the thinking of so many scientists. There is no evidence of any substance, subjective or objective. The only world that exists is a world of events. Events happen and then play a role in subsequent events. Are they "subjects" or "objects"? They are neither or both, since both terms point to aspects of reality but carry confused connotations derived from substantialist metaphysics. An event's happening is subjective in the sense that it is receptive of its past and exercises agency in relation to the future—it is a synthesizing of data, which have an objective character. The event is a datum for other events and, in that sense, an "object," as soon as it exists.

A moment of human experience is an event of this kind. It is a synthesizing of the data provided by the past into what is at once a new datum to be synthesized into others. Its basic pattern is similar to that of a quantum event: both culminate in a "decision." What is missing from modern thought is the act of synthesizing. This is what the dominant metaphysics excludes, but without that, there is nothing at all.

It is hard to exclude the language of object and subject. If we retain it, we can say that the subject is the act of synthesizing. The objects are all that is synthesized. They are inseparable. And as soon as the act is completed it becomes an object to be synthesized with other objects. If all science were reformulated on the basis of the primacy of events, the incongruity between the inherited science and quantum theory could be overcome.

The synthesizing includes the data or objects in a way that the data or objects do not include the synthesizing; so, if we use the language of subjects and objects at all, subjects are more fundamental. Therefore, I like very much a saying of Thomas Berry: "The universe is a community of subjects rather than a collection of objects."

3. Organisms Are Agents in Evolution

We have seen that long before Darwin, animal subjectivity was excluded from playing any role in the natural world on metaphysical grounds. It was this exclusion that made Darwin's theory such a threat to humanists. If animals have no subjectivity, or none that matters, and if humans are just another species of animals, then we have no subjectivity that matters. To defend the value and importance of human subjectivity, many humanists and religious people opposed Darwin. They wanted to maintain Cartesian dualism, which allows human beings to be treated respectfully as subjects responsible for their actions. If the view of other creatures did not change, the human status important to many required that human beings be a distinct creation. This could mean that at some point in physical evolution, God added a human soul.

This kind of effort to maintain human transcendence of nature continues to our day, sometimes with considerable political force. But among those who operate on the basis of evidence, the fact of evolution and its full inclusion of the human species has been decisively demonstrated. The serious issue now is whether the full acceptance of the evolutionary character of all things requires the exclusion of subjectivity.

Darwin himself left matters open. His contribution was to show how natural selection shaped the course of evolution. That it did so required that there be some variety among the members of the species that is evolving. It also required that there be some tendency for offspring to resemble their parents. But this did not exclude a role for purposive activity on the part of animals. Darwin was open to the idea of Lamarck that physical abilities developed by parents could be inherited by their children.

It turned out that genetics could provide an explanation both of the continuity and the variability required for evolution. The incorporation of genetics into evolutionary theory produced neo-Darwinism. Neo-Darwinists believed they had the full explanation of every aspect of evolution. The neo-Darwinian theory had the great advantage of assimilating evolutionary thinking into the preferred objectivist metaphysics. There was no need to consider animal actions.

Neo-Darwinism became overwhelmingly dominant among evolutionists. Evolution came to be regularly explained by the genetic diversity of offspring, with varying ability to survive long enough to reproduce. The inheritance of parental genes explained how some genes became more common in a population and led both to changes within a species and also the emergence of new species. Obviously, those herbivores that are genetically programmed to run faster are likely to outlast those who run more slowly in generation after generation. This selective principle applies equally to the predators. This explanation of increasing speed over the centuries and millennia is convincing.

However, the fact that a good many evolutionary developments are convincingly explained in this way does not justify the quick dismissal of other proposed contributions to evolution. This dismissal results more from the metaphysical assumptions than from any evidence.

Consider other ways in which evolutionary change may occur. For example, assume that the birds on some island eat worms, but that the supply of worms is limited and thus limits the bird population. Now suppose that edible worms live in holes in decaying trees that are deeper than the length of the beaks of the birds. Suppose that a bird picks up a pine needle, jabs it into a hole and pulls out a worm. Observing this, others copy. However, the beaks of many of the birds are not shaped well for the performance of this way of securing food. Previously, the variation in beaks had no evolutionary importance. Now certain genes are advantageous. This is likely to have an effect on which members of the species survive and thus on the genetic makeup of the species.

One who opposes introducing the intelligent action of animals into evolutionary theory might argue that the first bird to use the pine needle did so by accident. Perhaps. But in my view the repetition of this successful behavior and its imitation by others cannot be regarded as accidental. If this occurs, it is an instance of intelligent purpose playing a role in physical evolution.

When I have asked evolutionary biologists whether this kind of thing has occurred, most have agreed that it has. But I have noticed that the next time they explain how evolution has taken place, the contribution of intelligent action by animals is still not mentioned. A leading evolutionist, Richard Lewontin, wondered why animal behavior played so little role among his colleagues. The answer is clearly that it threatens their metaphysical assumptions.

The evidence is that the behavior of living things, omitted from neo-Darwinian theory, plays an important role among simpler organisms as well. Lynn Margulis devoted her career to the study of bacteria. She developed a theory about how eukaryotic cells emerged. These are the cells that make up our bodies and those of other multicellular creatures. Clearly their emergence was a major step in the evolutionary process.

Margulis found evidence that the eukaryotic cell contains remnants of other cells. To put it crudely, it emerged by one cell absorbing another without totally destroying it. This is very different from random mutation. At first she was ridiculed, but finally the evidence was too strong to oppose. Margulis thought that other evolutionary developments also occurred through what she called "symbiosis" rather than random mutation, but she had difficulty getting funds for research along these lines. In any case, the neo-Darwinists who continue to say that all evolution occurs by random mutation and natural selection now know that what may be the single most important step in the whole evolutionary process did not occur in this way. It is somewhat shocking that they typically fail to mention this fact.

Whereas Margulis experienced pressure *against* her discoveries, today there is a lot of research on the epigenetic elements in the cell. Like animal behavior and bacteria, the results are quite different from neo-Darwinian orthodoxy. It turns out that there are Lamarckian elements in evolution after all. If evolutionary biologists were not wedded to the objectivistic metaphysics, the cumulative evidence would have put an end to the simplistic mantra we hear so often. Neo-Darwinists could still explain that many evolutionary developments occurred as they have described, but no one would present random mutation as the only basis for providing the variations among which natural selection operates. Sadly, it seems that no amount of evidence suffices to end the dogmatic chant of the neo-Darwinists. What does not fit their theory they ignore.

They tend to treat their opponents as if they were all opposing scientific evolutionism. The continued efforts to support political opposition to the responsible teaching of evolution by appealing to pseudo-science and to biblical authority reinforce the metaphysical dogmatism of many scientists. On the other hand, their dogmatism in the face of contrary evidence fuels the opposition to their control of what is taught. It would be a wonderful breakthrough if all could agree to be guided by the evidence.

I have limited myself to the discussion of how evolution occurs. Of course, there are many other dimensions to the study of living things, and it is my impression that the more we learn, the greater is the feeling of wonder at the remarkable characteristics of all of them. Once we remove our reductive assumptions, living things display capabilities as subjects that far exceed our expectations. Today we talk quite straightforwardly of how they communicate information among themselves. Bacteria have "memory"; plants respond to human emotions; the planet as a whole displays signs of "intelligence." I hardly know what all this means, but I am quite sure that once the bondage of scientists to a bad metaphysics ends, science will flourish in a world of subjects.

I commend the writings of a thoroughly open-minded biologist, Rupert Sheldrake, who asks scientists to test theories that clearly challenge their metaphysics. Thus far the scientific establishment has excommunicated him and refuses to discuss his theories. They seem to know that if they tested his theories, the rug would be pulled out from under their orthodoxies. Therefore, the response is to silence and ignore.

4. Human Subjects Are Agents Too

I have told the story of how neo-naturalism lost out, because it is important for us to know that the victory of its opponents was not based on argument or evidence. Just as the original victory of the mechanistic model was not based on serious debates about its merits, so its subsequent victory over the new naturalism does not mean that the alternative view was rejected by strong arguments or empirical evidence.

In this book our focus is on God. I have noted that the role of God in the world cannot appear as long as subjective experience is rejected as explanatory of what happens. Accordingly, the first stage of the reinstatement of a divine role in natural events must be the reinstatement of subjects. After we have done that, we can ask whether there is specific indication that one of the subjects that participate in the explanation of what happens is Abba.

For the neo-naturalists, the fact that we know ourselves to be subjects with feelings and purposes is sufficient grounds to assert that feelings and purposes are part of nature. Further, we really cannot doubt that our feelings and purposes affect our actions and thus affect what happens in the natural world. Hence we know that we cannot agree to the denial that subjective experience plays a causal role in the natural world. To us, this situation by itself offers adequate reason to oppose the assumptions that reign in the university.

However, we must take seriously all efforts by the supporters of the university orthodoxy to justify their doctrines. This effort is most sharply focused in neuroscience. Defenders of orthodoxy know that we subjectively feel that our decisions affect what we do. The orthodox view is that our feelings, including the feeling of making a decision, are epiphenomenal. That is, the actual causes are all to be found in the neurons. Our subjective feelings are products of the neuronal activity. They have no causal effect on what happens. The course of objective events would be the same if we had no subjective feelings.

A full explanation of human experience in terms of this kind of orthodoxy would become stranger and stranger. But let us take matters quite simply. Can scientists show that our feelings, including the feeling of deciding, are caused by neuronal activity? This is the task assigned to neuroscientists by the scientific establishment. No one doubts that our subjective experience is affected by our bodily condition. We feel the ache in our teeth, the bodily need for rest, the stimulating effect of a cup of coffee. Ordinary experience settles for most people the question of whether the physical condition of the body has an influence on subjective experience.

Accordingly, there is no surprise when neuroscience supplies more detailed information about the effects of neuronal events on subjective experience. But common sense does not agree that because some subjective experiences are caused by neuronal events, this is true of all. This is what the defenders of orthodoxy want neuroscience to prove, and they assume that it is just a matter of further research to complete the task. This is similar to the situation of science on many topics; it never supplies the total explanation of any event. But it has explained a great deal and we are expected to assume that it can and will explain still more.

In neuroscience this expectation is becoming less and less plausible. Neuroscientists know that they are expected to provide evidence of the determination of subjective experience by what they can study objectively in the brain. But their experiments in fact show that there is influence in both directions. Not only does neuronal activity affect subjective mental states, but subjective states also affect the brain.

The most impressive evidence comes from research on those who meditate seriously, especially Buddhists. It turns out that this meditation actually affects the growth in size of parts of the brain. We may, of course, claim that the decision to meditate and the actual meditating are entirely explicable in terms of objective brain events. But this is clearly blind faith. Any account of the evidence that is "objective" in the sense of open-minded and metaphysically neutral will attribute objective events to subjective ones as well as subjective events to objective ones.

In one sense this only confirms what we have known all along. We decide to stand up and we stand up. Our experience is that the subjective decision plays an important role in determining which movements of the body will take place. Of course, this does not exclude the fact that our reason for standing up may have been physical discomfort or hunger. But orthodox scientists have been convinced that the causal relationship goes only one way, and that attributing causal efficacy to subjects is illusory and naïve—or "unscientific." They have been sure that more rigorous experiments would show that our subjective feeling of deciding is "epiphenomenal." That is, they believe that the subjective experience of decision is a byproduct of objective events and plays no role in them. Most self-respecting moderns have thought that they must be "tough minded" and follow the lead of the scientists. So despite common sense and the scientific evidence supporting it, the objectivist view plays a large role in most academic disciplines and in the modern value-free research university as a whole.

Accordingly, the experimental evidence supporting our naïve views that our thinking and deciding make a difference is of great importance. It threatens the assumptions underlying the modern value-free research university as a whole. If subjective experience plays a causal role in the objective world, then science needs dramatic reform. In particular, modeling the study of human beings on the Cartesian study of nature loses any justification.

Scientists are torn between two aspects of modern science. One aspect is the attachment to objectivist metaphysics. That is, most scientists have been socialized to think that the sort of things experienced visually and by touch are the only "real" things. That is, they are the only things that can enter into a valid explanation of what happens. These scientists have been taught that to allow anything like a human decision to be employed in explanation is to be unscientific.

The second aspect of modern science is the view that the task of science is to test all theories against experience. Many believe that a theory that is in principle untestable does not belong to science. They also believe that science should follow all the evidence and not dismiss it because it is inconvenient or fails to support their preferred theories.

Today the evidence does not support the metaphysics. Thus far the dominant community has chosen to retain the metaphysics and ignore or deny the evidence. But those of us who do not accept the metaphysics have no obligation to support them in this choice. We favor a science that takes account of all the evidence. We realize that political power is in the hands of those who favor the metaphysics against the evidence, but we think we should not be intimidated from urging that science adjust to evidence.

5. Subjects Do Some Remarkable Things

The field of research that most directly opposes the dominant metaphysics is the study of "psy" phenomena or parapsychology. Psy phenomena are those that show communications between entities or the effects of mental states on entities that do not employ physical means. Mental telepathy or mindreading without sensory signals is a major form, and affecting physical objects by mental means without physical contacts is another.

The main reason for believing that this takes place is that there are so many reports of occurrences that seem to require this explanation. Some individuals seem to have extraordinary psychic powers. There are many stories of this kind in ancient traditions and sacred writings, and what we call "faith healings" are frequently reported. Few doubt that they can raise the temperature of their fingers by mental concentration. It is a common observation that dogs seem to know when their masters are coming home without sensory cues.

Scientists tend to discount this kind of evidence, even when long lists of individual instances are compiled. There are never enough controls to exclude other explanations. Hence believers have gone to great length to establish laboratories that are well controlled and to engage in experiments there.

The results of these experiments are typically very tame in comparison with the reports that create the excitement. It is probably the case that the sterile context of the laboratory does not encourage the sort of emotion and thinking that are associated with dramatic instances. Nevertheless a few subjects achieve remarkable results even under these circumstances, and the overall results are often statistically significant. If scientists approached matters neutrally, they would agree that in the world of subjects causal relations have been shown to be possible without physical intermediaries.

But many scientists reject the possibility a priori on metaphysical grounds and assume that there must be errors in the experiment even if they cannot find them. Since no amount of care can overcome this metaphysical objection, laboratories at universities have largely disappeared. We are left with ordinary observation and reports from more and less reliable sources.

At the same time that most scientists do not believe that there can be mental communication between people without sensory cues or some kind of field connecting them, they now have to deal with quantum phenomena in which something like action at a distance is taking place. This can be obscured by language like "quantum entanglement," but it cannot be denied. If progress is made toward understanding large-scale entities in terms compatible with the behavior of the quantum world, the a priori exclusion of mental telepathy will fade. Meanwhile those of us who do not share the objectivist metaphysics need not be limited to the evidence that meets the metaphysical demands of so many scientists. We can take subjective experience seriously and learn about its transcendence of the objectivist world from normal life and experimental verification.

It is striking that in recent years much of the evidence has focused on the effects of emotions. Many people have participated in experiments in blessing and cursing plants. The results are often quite dramatic. Individual cells and even molecules seem to be affected by human emotions. Our common experience of sensing the mood of a crowd need not be reduced to sensory cues. We need not suppose that the effects on us of another's hatred and anger are entirely based on our interpretation of sense data.

In these cases there may be some kind of field in which we exist along with others that is directly affected by emotion. The issue of when this is action at a distance is a separate matter. If subjective experience is involved with emotional fields that have emotional effects on others, this is a large topic, thus far excluded from science. Once the subjective side of reality is given equal attention with the objective, new sciences will flourish.

6. Abba's Role as Subject and in Subjects

Our interest in this book is in God. Most of this chapter has been a long excursus on subjectivity. The reason is that it is meaningless to talk about God if subjects play no role in the world. God is certainly not an object of vision or touch or anything analogous to that. If serious and honest thinkers are required by evidence and good reasoning to adopt the objectivist metaphysics, then God cannot play a role in the world, and a "being" that plays no role in the world is not "God" in the Abrahamic sense.

I have explained my judgment that the objectivist metaphysics was never correct and that the reasons for supporting it even provisionally are no longer valid. It prevents us from dealing well with a vast body of evidence. In my judgment, this fundamental reason for excluding God has crumbled.

The claim that subjects play a role in the world opens the door to including God as a player. Also the kind of role that subjects play is suggestive of where God might be found. This brings us back to the sort of roles discussed under the heading of "Personal Experience of Abba" in chapter 3. When we dethrone objectivism, my claim to experience God in the call forward cannot be dismissed a priori.

If we have grounds for claiming that God participates in human experience and affirm our evolutionary continuity with other living things, we have reason to expect that God participates in their experience as well. The philosopher Alfred North Whitehead wrote that all living things aim to live, to live well, and to live better. Why is the world like this? When we find something that is true universally, it is reasonable to suppose that there is a common reason.

The discovery of a call forward in ourselves suggests that everything that lives is called to live, to live well, and to live better. If the one who calls me is God, it is reasonable to think that the one who calls all things is God. And this gentle caller, who lures and does not force, is best understood as Abba. Abba seeks the realization of intrinsic value. This is Abba's working in us, and it is Abba's working in all living things. Indeed, it is Abba's working in every individual thing.

Intrinsic value is the quality of subjectivity. If it were not for Abba, there would be no reason for the universe to produce and promote organisms. From a value-free point of view a dead universe is as good as one that supports life—perhaps better. There are some today who seem to think that a world of robots might be an improvement over a world of living things. They are correct that it would be much less messy, and suffering could be eliminated. But the cost would be the elimination of all feeling, and creatures who could not suffer would be of far less intrinsic value. If we are responsive to Abba's call to us, a call always to achieve as much value as possible, we will do all we can to reduce the assault on the biosphere, an assault in which all of us now participate.

7. An Infinity of Universes or One Subject?

Perhaps the deepest reason that even those who recognize the role of subjects in the world do not want to introduce God into the picture is the difficulty of identifying what works individually, and even personally, in our lives with something that plays a role in the whole cosmos. This was already noted as a marvel by the ancient Hebrew psalmist (Psalm 8:4). How can the creator of heaven and earth be interested in something as minor as human beings, and especially individual human beings? Since that time, the problem has greatly intensified, as the cosmos of which we are aware has expanded incomprehensibly. The heavens and earth the psalmist considered are a trivial part of a galaxy, which has a minor role in a cluster of galaxies, and so forth, and so on.

If we seem to find on the Earth and in ourselves an urge or lure toward the realization of value, and if we feel that this comes from something that is both within us and present everywhere, that is, a cosmic Spirit, what would we expect cosmologists to find? We would expect that where the conditions allow, life appears. Someday space exploration may give us answers as to whether that occurs, but for now it is simply a hypothesis that can in principle be tested, but not yet actually.

No one can deny that the basic structure of the universe allows for life. Until recently that did not seem especially remarkable, but cosmologists have now discovered that this is far more significant than most theists had supposed. They have found that so far as they can tell, the universe could easily have been inhospitable. Indeed, viewing matters from a detached perspective, the chances of its being hospitable were very small, even infinitesimal. They recognize that it is *as if* a choice had been made among myriads of options for the one that allows for life.

I have noted that evolution brought about a shift from deism to atheism. Before the evolutionary character of the world was understood, people could not imagine how the present world with all its complexity came into being without the action of a powerful intelligence. The evolutionary vision indicated that this complexity could arise by natural processes from a much simpler condition. God was no longer needed to explain the origin of the world.

But now the further study of things has not gone in the anticipated direction. Science has not found a few simple entities and principles from which all the complexity derived. I recently read an article titled "The Big Seed: It Takes 26 Fundamental Constants to Give Us Our Universe, but They Still Don't Give Everything." The effort to develop theories that would account for all this on simpler principles continues, but thus far the search has led to greater complexity. Perhaps the world needed a powerful and intelligent creator after all!

Actually the reasons for such a move are very strong. A characteristic of a constant is that there is no explanation of its being what it is. So far as scientists can see, it could be different. Yet in many cases, if the constant were even a little different, the universe could not contain life. Indeed, scientists are more and more impressed by the fact that a life-supporting universe is exceedingly improbable. Its likelihood among all the equally possible universes is infinitesimal. The simplest explanation is that a very powerful and very intelligent being shaped the universe so that life could emerge. The deists of the early modern period would feel fully vindicated.

Many scientists agree that when we consider just the evidence about the low probability of the occurrence of the conditions that make life possible, it is *as if* purposeful intelligence played a role. But still, most scientists reject this explanation, and by now we understand why. Scientists are conditioned to reject any introduction of purpose or decision into their explanations. Their task, determined by the metaphysics they take to be sacred, is to find an explanation that does not involve a decision, and in particular, a divine decision.

The only option seems to be "chance." Out of a trillion possible universes, by chance the one that came into being is the one that supports life. Such a statement can never be refuted, but scientists have been trained not to make such moves lightly. With regard to most scientific theories, alternative possibilities exist. It is rare that a theory is *proved* in the sense that no alternative explanation is *possible*.

For example, you could almost always posit that all the samples or instances studied in developing the theory had, by chance, a particular characteristic that supported the theory, but that many not selected lack this characteristic. No number of tests could exclude this possibility. But at some point, the failure to discover any exceptions leads to the conclusion that there are none.

Scientists are not much worried by the abstract possibility that chance explains their data. Once the chance of error is sufficiently small, they consider their theory proved. That they do not follow this procedure in the case of the life-supporting character of the universe is due to the nature of the proffered explanation. It introduces intelligent purpose into the account, and this is unacceptable. On the other hand, simply to say every time new evidence appears for intelligent choice that it is a matter of chance is, to say the least, an uncomfortable position for scientists.

Accordingly, theories are now being propounded about a vast multiplicity of universes. If there are a trillion universes, we could expect that one of them would be hospitable to life. That we living beings inhabit that one requires no further explanation.

I trust the reader knows not to take my "trillion" seriously. Exact calculations of probabilities in such a matter are not significant. I intend only to indicate a *very* large number, large enough to cause consternation in the atheist community. Whereas many scientists once opposed theories for which no test can be imagined, it turns out that the theory of multiple universes can be taken quite seriously without the question of testability being seriously raised. The avoidance of God as an explanatory factor takes precedence over everything else.

However, we may still ask for clarification as to just what is meant by multiple universes and just what character they must have to provide a serious theory. Less attention has been given to these questions than we might expect. The problem is that the theory requires radical disconnection between the universes. Discovering another cluster of clusters of galaxies would not do. It would only enlarge the size of *this* universe unless the constants in that newly discovered cluster were different from those in the universe we know. But all our instruments and calculations depend on the universe we know. So we must posit without any evidence that these other universes differ in their constants from ours and from one another.

On the other hand, if the universes were too different from ours, then they would cease to help in the calculations of probability. For example, if we suppose some of them contained nothing that we would recognize as physical energy, their existence would not reduce the improbability of ours. Some of the Indian visions include myriads of spiritual universes, but these would not help. The calculation of the probability of the constants has to be based on universes somewhat like ours but with different constants.

Some who realize the difficulty of coexisting universes, sufficiently like ours to count in the calculation but differing in the relevant respects, prefer to posit a temporal succession of universes. This is easier to conceive, since most scientists now believe our universe had a temporal beginning. It is reasonable to think that the Big Bang may have followed upon a Big Crunch. This universe in turn may end in another such Crunch. In infinite time, there could be an infinite number of universes.

If the temporal sequence of universes is to serve to reduce the marvel of our own, the problems are similar to those noted above. We must posit that they are all much like ours but with different constants. This is itself somewhat improbable. But we may be satisfied by the response that in infinite time there will be infinite universes and all things will be possible.

However, that there will be an infinite succession of universes is particularly improbable. For this to happen each must conclude in a Big Crunch. But it seems quite uncertain whether even our universe will stop expanding and begin to condense toward a Big Crunch. If it does not, the idea that it will still be succeeded by another beggars the imagination. But let it be supposed that this universe will end in a Big Crunch out of which comes another Big Bang producing a universe that meets the requirements of similarity and difference. It would be truly remarkable if with all their other differences, in an infinite sequence none ever failed to end in a crunch. We would then have another infinitely improbable view of the whole sequence of universes to explain as chance by more infinites.

Does this prove that there has been a divine decision favoring the actualization of value? No, there is no proof. Someday scientists *may* come up with an explanation they can regard as "scientific." It is impossible to disprove that things happen by chance. But there is an explanatory hypothesis against which there is no evidence. It is a hypothesis proposed on the basis of a plausible explanation of our experience. What we find at the cosmic level is coherent with what we find in our experience. The same general hypothesis fits well with the facts of biology and evolution. For me this is enough. I believe there is a cosmic Spirit that aims at the increase of value. It works as we would expect the Abba of Jesus to work. Apart from the arbitrary metaphysical prohibition, the probability in favor of this account is enormous. For me this is sufficient.

8. Can the Metaphysical Prejudice Be Shaken?

One of the most clearsighted and honest scientists is the respected biologist Richard Lewontin. He recognizes that the evidence points to a divine decision, but he says that scientists cannot follow that evidence, because if God gets a foot in the door, that is the end of science. What makes him think that?

Perhaps he supposes that to believe in God is to posit a being outside the world who has the power to interfere in worldly events. Some theists no doubt have images of that kind in their minds. To believe that would certainly create problems for science. It would mean that alongside the normal law-abiding occurrences there were others that violated the laws of nature. How they would fit into the ongoing course of events is hard to imagine. Science would certainly be disrupted in serious ways.

However, few serious theists today support this kind of thinking. It belongs much more to the polytheism that theism undertook to displace. God is thought of far more as the source and guarantor of natural order than as one who violates it.

On the other hand, many Christians, and even what is regrettably regarded as orthodox theology, do teach divine omnipotence. It is my assumption that many scientists suppose that introducing God into the causal system is giving a place to One who controls everything. They assume that God is an all-powerful being whose actions follow from purposes that are not accessible to us. Scientists who acknowledge this God's role in the world then have no further ability to specify what is possible and impossible, for everything is possible for God. Events may or may not follow natural laws or statistical generalizations.

For scientists to suppose that the doctrine of omnipotence has been used in the past to damage science in this way shows a sad ignorance of history. Prior to the controversies over Darwin, most scientists believed in God and attributed to God the basic principles of order found by science. Indeed, it was the belief that God was rational and powerful that inspired many early scientists to seek regularities in the midst of surface variety. To suppose that attributing the life-supporting constants to God would end science is simply false.

Nevertheless, we must take the concern seriously. Reintroducing God into the causality of natural order does imply that subjective elements such as purpose and decision have causal power. The deists assumed that this was the case both with respect to human beings and God. Contemporary scientists have been socialized to exclude subjectivity from the causal realm as their ancestors in science were not. I have devoted much of this chapter to this topic. I believe there are many reasons other than belief in God for scientists to rethink this exclusion. Once we all agree to acknowledge the role of subjective experience in the course of events, we can sharpen the issues about God.

To allow for subjectivity to play a role in what is objectively observed is simply to follow the evidence. But in relation to creaturely subjectivity it is possible to study empirically what it can and cannot do. Science will be enriched when it finally turns attention to these questions.

Just as it is possible to indicate the ways in which creaturely subjective experience affects what happens as well as its limits, so also such distinctions can be made with respect to Abba. Earlier in this chapter, I proposed that we understand each act of experiencing as a synthesizing of the past world. Abba has a role in each act. Abba offers to the experiencing occasion the possibility that will achieve the greatest value in that particular situation. This in no way does away with the consequences of the past. The act of experiencing is always experience of a given past that cannot be changed. God introduces a certain freedom into the occasion, but that only has to do with how the past is synthesized, not with whether that past will play a determinative role in the outcome.

The "laws of science" will not be broken. But when we view any situation in full detail, these "laws" do not determine exactly what will happen. Much can be predicted, but the idea that everything to the last detail can be predicted has always been a matter of faith, never of demonstration. As we have learned more about quantum phenomena, the metaphysical faith in exact predictability has been abandoned.

The evidence is that there is novelty, freedom, purpose, and responsibility in the world. The effort to deny all that has failed, and insisting on this denial will increasingly damage the authority of science. God is the source of novelty, freedom, purpose, and responsibility. Acknowledging this divine contribution will not reduce the predictive power of science. It will, of course, be a recognition that science, too, is limited. It can predict important aspects of the future, but not all. Neither science nor God knows what will happen in every respect. That has always been the situation in the past, and that will always be the situation in the future. A science that presents the situation realistically will be an improvement over one that pretends to potentials it does not have and cannot have. If science will become open to evidence and to supporting the most probable implications of that evidence, it can regain the respect that some of its more arrogant representatives have sometimes caused it to lose.

5

Does Abba Call for Christian Exclusivism?

In the preface, I mentioned some of the crimes that have been committed in the name of Christianity. I am quite sure that if Christians had always worshiped Jesus' Abba our record would not be as bad. I hope that some of the difference is apparent. However, there are those Christians who think that centering our lives on Jesus and Jesus' beliefs is inherently damaging to relations with other religious communities, especially if we make strong claims for the desirability of what we are doing. I want to make the case that advocating for devotion to Abba need not have this effect. I hope, indeed, that this may strengthen relations with other faith communities. This chapter sketches my hopes.

1. Abba and Deep Pluralism

Ours is an age of pluralism. Whereas people have always known that there were those who thought and acted quite differently, the usual view was that they were eccentric. Normal people believed and acted like "us," whoever the "us" might be.

But today, the others are all around us. It is no longer so clear who "we" might be. Some respond to this situation by identifying strongly with some "we" and defining it tightly. We call this response "fundamentalism." The term applies especially to a reactionary Protestant movement. But this is only one form of fundamentalism. There are secularist forms of fundamentalism as well as religious ones. The most dangerous fundamentalism today is nationalism, especially in the form of "American exceptionalism."

The most common alternative is one that minimizes the importance of beliefs and even communities. It holds that individuals should work out matters of this sort for themselves, that whatever they conclude is fine as long as they don't try to impose it on others. Live and let live.

In this libertarian context, there is no place for theologians. Our job has been to sort out different claims to truth and commend some as superior to others. To this extent, we violate the principle of live and let live. We may be very careful not to be aggressive in presenting our ideas about better and worse beliefs, but we cannot accept the idea that we should be entirely quiet. This book is unabashedly commending one way of thinking about God over against rejecting God altogether and also against thinking of God in other ways.

Some libertarians accept the legitimacy of engaging in such discussion within a community of belief but oppose introducing it into the discussion with those who are not part of that community. They note the long history of mutual condemnation of communities. In the relation between communities, they oppose any claims that imply the superiority of one over others.

They have much justification for opposing statements of this kind. In the pluralistic context, mutual respect is very important. Claiming that one community has a truth that others lack can be disrespectful. Still, I am promoting the affirmation of Jesus' Abba. Does this cut against the mutual respect that is so important? My view is that it does not, or, at least, need not.

To make the case that I can urge devotion to the Abba of Jesus without violating the principle of mutual respect, I need to consider the meaning of mutual respect more deeply.

Sometimes the call for mutual respect suggests that we should not assert anything as true that adherents of other communities deny. We are pushed to limit ourselves to the most commonplace beliefs. But to me it seems that those who push me in that way are not showing respect for my beliefs. My experience in interfaith dialogue has been that my dialogue partners want me to assert my Christian beliefs clearly, as I certainly want them to assert their Muslim or Buddhist beliefs clearly. I welcome their criticisms of my belief and they often welcome my criticism of theirs.

There is a place for seeking a common platform for working together. This often has great practical importance, but it is not dialogue. Liberal Protestants who want to assure their dialogue partners that they don't believe any of the things that have made Christianity distinctive can contribute very little to dialogue. Indeed, I consider their program to be an obstacle to dialogue.

Mutual respect cannot mean that we hold that every opinion is worthy of equal respect. Calling for mutual respect implies that we do not fully respect fundamentalist opinions when they block mutual respect. But it also means we will not expect others to give up their beliefs just because we do not share them, and we will expect them to respect our adherence to our beliefs as well.

If we really respect one another, as is usually the case in dialogue groups, we will often try to persuade others of beliefs that they have not derived from their own traditions. But we do this respectfully only if we are open to learning from the others, gaining insights that we have not derived from our tradition. If something seems to me to be both true and universally important and I keep silent about it, I am not showing real respect for my partner. Equally, if I reject my partner's insights just because they do not fit comfortably into the position with which I enter the dialogue, I am not showing real respect.

It is also true that some beliefs set inexorable limits to dialogue. That is, we may hold to some beliefs that require that we press them on our dialogue partners, because they are thought to be essential to their ultimate well-being. We may respect those who on such grounds turn from dialogue to conversion, but we also should recognize that this is a rejection of pluralism and of the relationships supported by pluralism.

For example, suppose that a Christian believes that Anselm correctly formulated the nature of Christian faith. *God could forgive us only if God in human form paid the price for our sins. Believing that Jesus' death has redeemed us is the heart of our faith. Those who do not believe this are destined to eternal punishment.* A sincere belief of this kind leads people to try to save the other person. We may admire those who make great personal sacrifices in the effort to do this. To put forth these beliefs cannot be a basis of dialogue. Of course those who believe these things can be humanly respectful toward those who do not, and indeed their efforts to convert them may express deep concern for them. But dialogue requires a kind of mutuality that this kind of belief precludes.

If I thought that my strong affirmation of Abba inherently hindered dialogue, I would be deeply distressed. It is my hope that I can show that the acceptance of my belief is not incompatible with the central and indispensable beliefs of my dialogue partners. In other words, the sort of pluralism that I affirm is one in which the deepest convictions of all are not such as to require the rejection of the deepest convictions of others. I call this deep pluralism. I enter conversation with adherents of other faiths with the assumption that their traditions could not have survived and won the loyalty of millions of people over time if they did not embody important truths. I disagree with those who suppose that our traditions are all paths up the same mountain or multiple ways of expressing the same truths. In some instances this may be correct, but anticipating this usually leads to failure to hear much of what is being said.

My goal is to formulate the implications of faithfulness to Jesus' Abba in such a way that persons in other great faith traditions will not find any of what I say impossible to accept. They may still think that other foci of attention and effort are more important than this one. They may not even be convinced of the reality of Abba. But they will see that to affirm Abba does not necessarily involve rejection of anything basic to their own tradition.

Please understand that the goal is not to avoid controversy. I will spend some time arguing that there is within Buddhist traditions an experience of an Other Power that is very much like the Christian's experience of Abba. But that strand of Buddhism is controversial within Buddhism. My reason for highlighting this is not that I thereby prove the accuracy of my views or show that Buddhists should accept them. The point is only that since this strand shares fundamental ideas with other Buddhists, the affirmation of Abba does not in itself deny the truth of fundamental Buddhist principles. In some traditions, the denial of God is quite central. I need to show that the "God" whose denial is important to that tradition is not Abba. This does not prove Abba's reality. But it means that we can affirm both Abba and the fundamental principles of Buddhism without contradiction.

I believe that I am called to witness to Abba and to the importance of devotion to him. I also believe that Abba calls me to listen to what persons from other traditions have to say and to be open to learning from them even what seems not to fit with my Christian tradition. I believe that what I learn from them helps me better to understand Abba and that the acceptance and affirmation of Abba would enrich those who have not previously attended to him. I hope that my claims about Abba will never be felt as an attack upon the deep truths of other wisdom traditions. I remain open to others following Abba under other names with or without knowledge of Jesus. But I confess my dependence on Jesus and encourage attention to his witness to Abba on the part of those in other traditions.

The topic of the chapter is often formulated as the Christian doctrine of other religions. This formulation is understandable but it has caused a great deal of confusion. It assumes that there is something called "religion" that can be found in all cultures, and that we can specify the communities or traditions that qualify for this label. Once we have classified these, we already know a lot about them. For example, we may think we know that they are all seeking salvation. Christians believe that salvation is gained by believing in Jesus. We can compare this answer with that of other religions. Such comparison rarely functions as a good discussion starter for real dialogue, because it has stacked the deck in advance.

If we start this way, the first answer would seem to be that the other religions are mistaken and that our task is to convert their members so that they may be saved. In fact Christians have acted, and many still act, on this basis. However, thoughtful Christians saw that there was much of value in these "other religions." Perhaps they also offered ways to salvation. This view is often called "religious pluralism."

The image that fits this teaching best is that of a mountain that can be climbed in different ways. Each religion offers a path up the mountain. Each should respect all the others as offering other valid paths.

Religious pluralism has been popular among liberals who

recognize the need for mutual respect among the great traditions. But it has turned out to be profoundly unsatisfactory. The idea of "religion" has no equivalent in non-Abrahamic cultures. Its imposition is yet another example of colonialism. When people in these other cultures hear that they are offering a path to salvation, they want to know what is meant by "salvation." Abrahamic traditions sometimes focus on a decisive difference between two states of being after death. Other traditions may have no place for anything like that.

It turns out that what is often called "religious pluralism," by forcing a miscellaneous group of communities into a single rubric, is not adequately pluralistic. To have a single stance toward all the communities we place under this heading does not make sense. Christianity is related to different communities in different ways. For example, the relationship to Judaism is one of child to parent. The relation to Confucianism is entirely different.

Also, not all Christians have the same goal. Some may seek to go to heaven when they die, whereas others seek to advance the work of God's kingdom on earth. Few Hindus seek either of those goals. We are not all climbing the same mountain.

A true pluralism requires that each community describe itself in its own way. Christians will respond to each community by seeking to understand it and appreciate it in its own terms. Our response to Islam will be very different from our response to Taoism.

What are generally thought of as "religions" in discussions of "religious pluralism" are products of what Karl Jaspers taught us to call the Axial period, which occurred around two and a half millennia ago. Quite remarkably in China, India, Persia, Greece, and Palestine, individual thinkers arose who developed ideas about reality and human life that had universal meaning. The insights that emerged in that period continue to provide the grounds of profound reflection to the present time. They are all quite distinct and make different contributions to us, but they also have some common traits that distinguish them from other cultural forms and communities. We can call them all "wisdom traditions" without distorting their own understanding of themselves.

In a single chapter it is impossible to discuss them all. Significant sampling will have to do. I have referred several times to the Abrahamic family, the major members of which are Judaism, Christianity, and Islam. Its origins go back much further than the Axial period, but it is the prophetic tradition to which it gave rise during the Axial period that has the most importance for the present. In this section I will deal briefly with the relations of Jesus' Abba to Judaism and Islam.

This leaves out the many different wisdom traditions that developed in other parts of the world. Of these, I select Buddhism for special attention in the following section. The final section of this chapter will talk about how to relate to the many people who are not adherents of any of the wisdom traditions arising in the Axial period.

2. Abba and the Other Abrahamic Traditions

The most intense theological debates throughout the centuries have been in the Abrahamic communities. Most of these have been internal to individual communities. My primary purpose in this book is to propose that we look to Jesus for our doctrine of God rather than to Aristotle, Plato, Augustine, Anselm, Thomas, or Calvin. In chapters 1 and 2 I tried to show that this shift of focus is possible in Christianity, that it has played a positive role in the past, and that it can do so today. At least implicitly I have been arguing against other ways of thinking about God—ones that have also played important roles in the church. The question now is how would the shift from other ways of thinking of God in Christianity to focusing on Jesus' Abba affect our relations with the other Abrahamic traditions?

Some who may tend to agree with me may still be troubled, thinking that in our pluralist day, an emphasis on the specific contribution of Jesus is undesirable, that it hinders mutual respect among the Abrahamic faiths. I believe this is not the case, at least, not necessarily. To test this, let us remind ourselves of the common history I sketched in chapter 1.

The shared appeal to Abraham leads all three traditions to affirm a God who is not tied to any location or earthly powers. Instead these earthly rulers derive their authority or legitimacy from this God. This God calls for our wholehearted commitment.

All three traditions also accept the authority of Moses. He certainly affirmed the Abrahamic God. But whereas the God of Abraham does not seem to us very moral, the God of Moses is deeply concerned with morality. The Ten Commandments have provided a foundation of moral teaching in all the Abrahamic traditions. The uncompromising call for loyalty to this God, superseding all other loyalties, is even clearer with Moses than with Abraham.

The prophetic tradition from the eighth to the fifth centuries further develops the moral aspect of God and his transcendence over earthly authorities and geographical localities. More clearly than in Moses, there is a focus of attention on those who are oppressed by political and economic systems and by corrupt rulers. Justice trumps religious ceremonies and slavish obedience to written rules. The movement is toward emphasizing the motivation of actions and the transcendence of moral rules. In this period the idea that the God of Israel is the only real God was clearly established. This could support ideas of God's favoritism to the Jews, or it could be interpreted as emphasizing their responsibility to share with the world.

This tension was present in Jesus as well. His sense of mission led him to seek to save Israel from the self-destructive course on which it was embarked, but he was impressed that others responded to his message. He did not withhold from them, and after he died, his followers built on the universal aspects of his message. They created communities in which gentiles were on an equal footing with Jews, and because of their greater numbers, they soon became dominant. Jesus' Abba was known through the Spirit that was present in the churches.

In all of this, the followers of Jesus constituted a Jewish sect. Jesus' Abba was the God of Abraham, Moses, and the prophets. The prophets were seldom fully accepted in their own time, and Paul hoped that, as the Jews had posthumously recognized the authority of these prophets, so it would be with Jesus also. And so it might have been if the success among the gentiles had not so altered the movement that its Jewish identity itself was threatened.

Later, when Christianity became dominant, it adopted views that were explicitly anti-Jewish and the church often led in persecuting faithful Jews. Although the worst persecutions came later and were motivated by ethnic nationalism rather than theology, Christian teaching played a role even then. Urging Jews to "accept Jesus Christ" today usually means asking them to join a community with ideas deeply alien to Jews and sometimes explicitly anti-Jewish.

If the encouragement of Jews to consider the Abba of Jesus is taken as another form of this "evangelism," then it should be avoided. But it need not carry any of this baggage. Jesus was a Jew. Jesus' Abba was the God of Abraham, Moses, and the prophets. The affirmation of Jesus' Abba is quite possible for Jews. Indeed, many Jews have been devoted to the Abba of Jesus without any particular relation to Jesus. They are affected by many of the same traditions that affected Jesus.

This does not mean that no controversy is involved. The recommendation that Christians turn from the omnipotent judge of later Christianity to the Abba of Jesus is highly controversial among Christians. The recommendation that Jews turn from the legalistic, judgmental, nationalist God they often worship to the intimate, loving, universally accepting Abba of Jesus is certainly controversial among Jews. But it is an inner Jewish controversy and not one between Jews and the gentile church.

Although Jews may worship the Abba of Jesus without any special reference to Jesus, it is not wrong to hope that they will also affirm Jesus as a Jew who understood Abba in a peculiarly full and original way. For Jews to appreciate Jesus as a great Jew is not to abandon Judaism. Even the acceptance of Jesus as the "Messiah" is a possible move for Jews. "Jews for Jesus" have shown how far Jews today can go in honoring Jesus in Jewish categories.

We Christians must recognize that we continue to make this difficult for Jews. It is problematic for Jews to reclaim Jesus as a Jew as long as Christians claim ownership of Jesus and the prerogative to redefine "Messiah" as a person of the Trinitarian God. Paul hoped that the Jewish leadership would recognize that Jesus was the Messiah and then show gentiles what this truly meant. Perhaps we gentile Christians can now share in that hope. For us to seek to be faithful to the very Jewish God of Jesus might be a first step.

Islam is a different story. Whereas Jews took negative stands toward those who followed Jesus and in some official statements condemned Jesus, the Qur'an holds Jesus in great honor. It calls for respect for all "people of the book," which means all who stand in the Abrahamic traditions.

It is true that Muslims understand the Qur'an to supersede the sacred writings of Judaism and Christianity. The picture of Jesus in the Qur'an is quite different from that in the Christian scriptures. But the Qur'an still depicts a relation of Jesus to God that at least implicitly supports the idea of Abba that I am advocating.

This is not at all to say that calling for the worship of Jesus' Abba is uncontroversial in Islam. The images of God that have dominated Islam have been legalistic and imperial. But the Sufis are recognized as good Muslims, and they encouraged an understanding of God much like that of Jesus. To take sides with one strand of Islam rather than others is not to try to impose Christianity on Muslims.

The tone of these paragraphs may suggest that I am advocating significant efforts to intervene in discussions among Jews and among Muslims. I am not. I believe that the best contribution we Christians can make to the internal struggles of these other Abrahamic communities is to influence our own community to move in the direction of taking Jesus seriously.

I have written as I have in response to the fear on the part of liberal Christians that refocusing Christianity on Jesus would deepen the divides between Christians and other Abrahamic traditions. If this were likely, it would be a serious consideration in our pluralistic context. But I am convinced that this is not the case. Instead, downplaying later Christian dogma in favor of the historical Jesus can help even in the short run. These dogmas often obscure what is important about Jesus in the process of honoring him. We tell ourselves that our doctrines preserve the monotheism of the Abrahamic traditions, but Jews and Muslims are not so sure. However, no one has reason to suppose that Jesus deviated from monotheism. In the long run we might move toward a Christianity, a Judaism, and an Islam, all seeking to be faithful to Jesus' Abba. If that happened, the world would be a better place.

3. Abba and Buddhism

The Abrahamic traditions all seek to be faithful to the God of Abraham, Moses, and the prophets. I am proposing that all would gain if they understood God as Abba, as Jesus did. In each tradition, this would build on elements already present. We need now to ask whether this focus on a particular view of God would deepen the divide between the Abrahamic traditions and others. Pushing for taking Jesus seriously means siding with one possibility in our Abrahamic traditions instead of others. This is a controversy I do not want to avoid. My hope is that this controversy will bring us closer to our friends in other Abrahamic traditions rather than drive a wedge between us. But what about our relations to the wisdom traditions of China and India?

One of the great gains in the twentieth century was the discovery of these wisdom traditions that do not trace their origins to Abraham. Too often we approach these asking how they understand "God." This shows how deeply connected in our minds are "faith" and "God," and how quickly we assume that every advanced culture must have some way of dealing with these topics. We are only gradually overcoming this prejudice and listening to those who ask different questions.

If we now propose to emphasize a certain way of understanding God, derived from the Abrahamic tradition, what happens? Are we not alienating ourselves from those who ask different questions and find answers to which the Abrahamic "God" is irrelevant or worse? Should we not, instead, de-emphasize God and focus instead on the values that our several traditions share?

These are important questions. If our efforts to renew our Christian tradition end up moving us back to negative relations with other communities, perhaps it is better to just fade away. Perhaps a new syncretism can be born that would portend a better future for the planet. This book is not the place to explore this different strategy. But it is the place to discuss whether in fact an emphasis on "Abba" will alienate those with whom we seek companionship and mutual support. I dare to think it need not.

Now let me make clear that the versions of the Abrahamic God that have been most familiar to participants in the great traditions of China and India have typically been offensive. The developed orthodoxies of the theistic traditions often attribute omnipotence to the God of Abraham and declare that his creation of the world out of nothing is the essential mark of his deity. These ideas are not in the Bible, but even in the Bible there is a strand of thought that models God on earthly kings, only attributing to him even greater power. When we Christians commit ourselves to that line of biblical thinking and seek to make it central to our lives, we certainly drive a wedge between us and other faithful people.

Another biblical theme is that of God as the great Judge. This is based on associating faith in God with obeying divine laws. It encourages fear of punishment after death as motivation for obeying the teachings of the church here and now. If we Christians commit ourselves to that line of biblical thinking and seek to make it central in our lives, this will also drive a wedge between us and other faithful people.

But there is another theme that runs through the Bible as a whole, but is especially accented by Jesus. God is neither cosmic ruler nor moral judge. God is love. And Jesus proposes that the image of that love is the love of an infant's father, that is, "Abba." Control and judgment fade into the background; tenderness and unconditional acceptance are central. What happens when we emphasize faithfulness to Abba? Does that drive others away?

There is no simple answer to that. In Hinduism there are forms of devotion that have similarity to this, but the understanding of the deities in question does not have a background in monotheism. But this difference can invite conversation rather than simply lead to offense. We can find traditions in India that give considerable support to a Hindu equivalent to this kind of monotheism. Devotion to Jesus' Abba can be a respected alternative in the Hindu context.

The question is much more difficult in relation to Buddhism. Gautama was not concerned with the gods, but he believed that attachment to a God was an obstacle to the attainment of enlightenment. This enlightenment is an awakening, not to unity with a divine reality but to the full realization that there is no reality to awaken to. The efforts to relate Buddhist awakening to Christian mystical experience end up driving a wedge between Christian mystical experience and the biblical God.

This formulation can support the view that pushing for an Abba-centered life drives a wedge between us and Buddhists. It is easy to conclude that we do better to start with the experience of our mystics. We can follow Paul Tillich who called us to focus on "Being Itself," the God beyond the God of the Bible. Buddhists will not be satisfied that when we focus on being we truly understand the emptying of being that is really ultimate. But it may be possible to rethink Being Itself so that it becomes more like Emptiness Itself, which even empties itself of emptiness.

To many Christians the assertion that there is nothing at the base of things, no ground for our living, nothing to which we can be devoted, sounds depressing. We call this view "nihilism," and we find the results of Western nihilism distressing. But paradoxically, instead of being driven to despair, Gautama found peace, serenity, even bliss.

The quest ended in the end of questing. There is nothing to seek. What happens, happens. It can be accepted for what it is, whatever it is. The "we" who accept have no more reality than the ephemeral happenings we accept. There is nothing that separates us from them. There can be no rivalry or conflict—only compassion. There is nothing that limits us. We are completely free.

In ordinary experience we interpret the present in terms of past experience and expectations about the future. Gautama calls us to let all that go. Let the present be what it is. Be mindful of that. Hopes and fears blind us and distort our perception. Let them go.

Obviously, fully overcoming our habitual tendencies is not an easy matter. Gautama is seen as having done this, thus becoming truly enlightened, therefore, a Buddha. In the Buddhist understanding there have been others. And orienting our life in this direction by detaching ourselves from the desire of earthly things, such as possessions and fame, brings a measure of enlightenment, and thus, serenity. Failure to achieve total enlightenment does not mean that the Buddhist teaching of nonattachment and mindfulness are meaningless or without saving force.

None of this seems to involve God. For most Buddhists, what they understand Abrahamic believers to mean by "God" is irrelevant or, actually, an impediment. They tend to be opposed to belief in God. "God" is thought of as being just that kind of ultimate reality whose existence Gautama denied. God is something to which we attach ourselves, and such attachment is rejected. God is a product of conceptualization, and all conceptualization distorts reality. Buddhism often presents itself as not only nontheistic but also atheistic.

Despite all this, within Buddhism, something like Jesus' Abba appeared and has played a large role. The history is complex, but I will summarize it with respect to Japan. Buddhism entered Japan from Korea and China primarily as a monastic movement. The quest for enlightenment required a discipline and a lifestyle not possible for ordinary people. And even for those who practiced diligently, success was elusive.

There was a logic that suggested another possibility. The Enlightened One had enormous spiritual power and also perfect compassion. He could help ordinary people to find their way. Buddha nature, realized in the few, was also the universal reality obscured in all things.

The tradition made a distinction between two aspects of the Buddha-nature. There is the *Dharmakaya*, which is the full realization of the ultimate nothingness. There is also the *Sambhogakaya*, which is ultimate reality for us, that is, pure compassion.

Some Buddhists decided that instead of devoting themselves, almost hopelessly, to arduous practices to approach Buddhahood, they would trust the compassion of Buddha. Those who trust in that compassion believe that they are assured of life in the Pure Land, where enlightenment is readily available. In the meantime they live with assurance and such nonattachment and freedom from distortion as they are already granted.

In Japan, Zen Buddhists tend to consider Pure Land Buddhism a somewhat corrupted form, but they are a small minority. Most Japanese Buddhists belong to the Pure Land tradition. They, like Zen Buddhists, deny that they believe in God. But the God in whom they disbelieve is not the Abba of Jesus. Their experience of a compassion not their own working in them, expanding their own compassion and assuring them of fulfillment, is not unlike the Christian experience of the Abba of Jesus. Indeed, it is my belief that some Buddhists and some Christians have come by different routes to orient their lives to the one reality that Buddhists call "Amida" and Jesus called "Abba."

If we are willing to take that step, we may be ready to take another. For Buddhists of all stripes, the problem with faith in God is that it is a form of attachment or clinging. Advance in the spiritual life for Christians is sometimes formulated in terms of ceasing to be attached to any worldly object and clinging only to God. Buddhists are likely to affirm this as a good beginning, but the spiritual life gains as we give up attachment or clinging altogether. They call on us to cease to be attached or clinging to God.

The question for Christians is whether faith really involves attachment and clinging. It is certainly often described in these terms, but we may be able to learn something from Buddhists here. Perhaps really to trust God is not to cling to him but to be free to let go; perhaps clinging is an expression of limited faith.

We can marvel that some Buddhists reject the help of "Amida" and yet attain profound spiritual realization. This does not mean that those of us who believe God's grace is at work everywhere suppose that in fact it is absent from them. We can rejoice with Pure Land Buddhists that the cosmic compassion that we call "Abba" and they call "Amida" is always present. But certainly this does not mean to deny that these Buddhists seek its help.

Even Zen Buddhists are not quite as closed to God as their rhetoric sometimes suggests. This qualification shows up in discussions between Pure Land and Zen Buddhists. The contrast between them is often described by Pure Land Buddhists as the affirmation of Other Power on their part and Self Power by Zen. Some Zen Buddhists object. This formulation implies a dualism of self and other that they do not accept. Since they deny the reality of "the self," it is misleading to say they rely on "self power." The power on which they rely is the power of Buddha nature. Perhaps their reliance on Buddha nature is not so different, after all, from our reliance on Abba.

Let me be clear. What Buddhists deny is the reality of a cosmic person who decides the fate of all things and acts upon us from without. If that is what is meant by "God," then I share the Buddhist rejection of theism. I believe, however, in a cosmic Spirit that seeks our good and works within us and in all things to effect that good in us and in all things. Clearly that formulation comes from the Abrahamic traditions, and many Buddhist may find it objectionable.

But when they speak of the Buddha-nature *for us* and call it *Sambhogakaya,* when they describe this as pure compassion and trust it to save them, we can hardly fail to see connections with Jesus' experience of Abba and Paul's reference to the Spirit. The actual experience of Buddhists does not rule out our belief in the universal presence and working of Abba.

4. Abba and Indigenous Wisdom

The modern world has taught us to respect modern scientific knowledge as primary. It has allowed a secondary place for philosophy and a tertiary place for what we are calling the Axial thinkers. But still older forms of thought are dismissed altogether.

A few anthropologists studied tribes that have survived without becoming part of the modern world. They found that there were respects in which their ways of thinking made a great deal of sense. The door to appreciating the wisdom of our ancestors was cracked.

Finally, the ecological crisis led many to view civilization as such, and modern civilization in particular, critically. Total commitment to an unsustainable society did not make sense. There is obviously something wrong with the modern mind that produced and celebrated this unsustainability. Perhaps these "primitive" people had something we need, and this recognition changed the connotations of the word *primitive*. Indeed as the attitude changed from condescension to respect, *primitive* was replaced by other terms such as *primal*, or *indigenous*. Instead of dismissing all that indigenous elders taught their youth as "superstition," "civilized" people began listening to find within indigenous teaching a wisdom that has been lost in the course of history and especially in modernity.

Very few people want simply to replace what has been learned through the axial traditions and modern research with the beliefs of indigenous people. Even among these people there is considerable openness to new ways of thinking. But it is no longer possible to dismiss the evidence of indigenous experience. Does that evidence count against the Christian belief in the universality of Abba?

I recognize that my knowledge of indigenous wisdom is very limited. I know that the wisdom attained by indigenous people is in fact quite diverse. My generalizations may be quite naïve. Nevertheless, I consider it more responsible to hazard a few remarks than to omit this topic altogether.

Prior to the emergence of cities, people living in tribes and small villages felt themselves to be part of a complex community of diverse species of living things. They thought of the human species, or at least of their own communities, as having unique importance, and they used their tools and social capacities to enhance that well-being even at the expense of other species. Their communities were not always sustainable, and sometimes they wiped out other species. Nevertheless, they were far more respectful of other creatures and more aware of dependence upon them and of their interdependence. They understood that their task was more to adapt to what was given them than to reshape their environments. They respected the traditions inherited from their ancestors and transmitted them to their children. They understood their role as including responsibility in both directions.

In general, their beliefs were informed by their practical experience with one another and the physical environment, but also by their sense of unseen spirits. These were plural and diverse and diversely related to living things and special locations and ancestors. They felt themselves to be addressed by these spirits and aided by them, but sometimes also opposed or harmed by them. They felt no need to define these spirits or develop a coherent picture of their relations with one another. Among them some people had greater power in relation to these spirits than others, and often they used their superior ability to heal, but they could also use it to curse.

Healings might occur simply through spiritual means, by exorcism, for example. Sometimes moderns can understand how either a charismatic healer who inspires great faith or the group processes involved in exorcism accomplishes a healing. Healers often knew a great deal about the curative power of plants that they used. But sometimes exorcisms occur even today that seem inexplicable to the modern mind.

Indigenous people often have childrearing practices that differ greatly from ours. In some tribes the traditional wisdom is that infants should be in constant physical contact with adults at least through their first year. There is much evidence that those civilized groups that separate infants from contact at an early age have paid a high psychological price for doing so. In other instances also, indigenous practices express a wisdom based on experience over many generations.

For the purposes of this book, the question is whether we can discern the working of Abba in the forms of human life that dominated the planet for hundreds of thousands of years before the emergence of cities. The question is not whether people thought in the same terms as Jesus. Obviously, Jesus' understanding was shaped by centuries of Jewish life and thought. But we do ask whether Jesus' belief in a divine Spirit that is intimately involved in the life of everyone is compatible with what we know or conjecture about human experience throughout most of the time that *Homo sapiens* has existed.

There is, first of all, a general congeniality. Jesus' vision was focused on subjects and their relations. The problem encountered when we try to fit Jesus' beliefs into the modern world lies chiefly in the extreme modern focus on the primacy of the objective. Jesus was much closer to the indigenous thought-world that not only affirms the subjectivity of other physical living things but also subjects or spirits that are not tied so closely to particular physical things.

For Jesus, it was of great importance to identify within the spirit-world that one Spirit that works everywhere and always for good. This need grew out of his Jewish faith. There was nothing quite like that in indigenous wisdom. But the quest to clarify and identify is not excluded by indigenous experience. Instead, it can be seen to be anticipated here and there in individual experiences and tribal teachings. When Christians bring to indigenous peoples ideas about a cosmic moral judge or absolute ruler, it often grates on established sensitivity. But the story of Jesus sometimes finds an enthusiastic welcome. Some indigenous people have no difficulty speaking of the Great Spirit.

Listening to the wisdom of indigenous elders may help us to recover a balance between the objective and spiritual worlds, between the physical and the spiritual. This assistance can only be welcome to those who would worship Abba in thought and action. Affirming commitment to the Great Spirit of pure compassion will not harm our relations with indigenous people.

6

A World in Crisis Needs Abba

Thus far I have argued that the on to whom Jesus was totally faithful, the one he knew as Abba, is quite different from what most Christians have been taught to think of as "God." There are many reasons for being skeptical about the latter and even good reasons for opposing belief in such a being. These reasons don't apply to Jesus' Abba. I have suggested that affirming Abba would have important advantages. But I have felt driven to write the book out of a deeper motivation. Without Abba I could find little basis for hope, and Abba can help much better if he is understood and consciously served. This concluding chapter explains my conviction and my hope.

1. The Primacy of History

The Bible is a profoundly historical book. That, of course, does not mean that the facts are always accurately related. Some might say that it is a collection of legends and stories more than a "history." If a history is understood to be an accurate account of past events, this suggestion is valid.

My use of "history" is different. I consider a history to be a sequential account of meaningful events that locates them in relation to one another and to a beginning. If it does not report an end, it points to directions and possibilities for the future. It locates the present in relation to the purported past and the possible futures. This location determines the meaning of contemporary events and the calling of individuals to action.

Such a history is at best a spin on actual memories and available evidence. It may include elements that are purely invented or imagined. But it is ineffective if it has so little verisimilitude as to fail to convince. It differs from legends, not so much in the degree of accuracy as in its attempt to integrate the stories of the past into a single narrative. Obviously, the Bible does not complete the process of integration. In both testaments we find the same events reported in different, and often conflicting, ways.

Much work is left to later generations of readers. The Qur'an is one such integration, one that overcomes the chaos and confusion of the biblical library, but, of course, at a certain cost. If we put the sacred scriptures of Jews, Christians, and Muslims alongside those of other communities, their historical character at once becomes manifest. If we place the scriptures alongside philosophical writings, the contrast may be even more striking.

Particularly striking is that God has a history. This is true in several senses. First, God is involved in the human stories, shaping and directing them. God's actions at one time depend on previous divine actions and human responses. Expectations of God's further actions based on past actions shape present human actions. Second, the understanding of God changed, so that the ways God acted and the divine purposes have a different character at different times. Third, throughout, God's chief concerns relate to what is happening historically. God is interested in individuals, but usually this interest has to do with their historical roles.

This last point requires some qualifications. In the stories of Jesus, sheer compassion for individuals leads to concern for the alleviation of their suffering. Anticipations of this kind of individualism can certainly be found in the Hebrew Scriptures.

John the Baptist, Jesus, and Paul also called for individual repentance in a way that heightened such tendencies in the Hebrew Scriptures. Following Jesus or joining one of Paul's congregations was emphatically an individual decision. The followers of Jesus and the congregations of Paul were voluntary associations of a kind not common before. Of course, people had voluntarily met for social and even religious purposes. But for the most part the groups they constituted could be fully assimilated in the existing society. They did not affect the basic identity of their members. On the other hand, entering the *basileia theou* did redefine a person's role in Jewish society, and joining a Pauline congregation redefined her role in the Roman imperium.

But this was not "individual salvation" in the sense that later developed. It was a move from one life-determining context to another very different one. You did not first relate to God differently and then decide to join with others who had made similar changes. You changed your relation to God by becoming part of a community in which God's Spirit was dramatically and effectively present.

The new Pauline communities lived out of an understanding of history. They reread the scriptures they shared with the Jews in such a way as to understand themselves as the heirs of that history. For Paul it was important to understand the other Jews as also continuing heirs, but sadly his reading was lost, and Christians and Jews ordered their lives and communities by competing histories. The long-term consequences were disastrous for Jews in predominantly Christian countries, and now for Palestinians.

Historical thinking has had other terrible consequences. In the Hebrew Scriptures it often justified vicious acts against those who did not worship the Jewish God. In Christianity it often led to supposing that God had chosen the Christian community and that its expansion was inherently good. The evil consequences of this idea were long checked by Jesus' teaching against violence, and for centuries Christians assumed that violence was never supported by their faith. But this check ended when Charlemagne persuaded his bishops to preach that God would reward those who killed the enemies of the church. From then on the historical consciousness gave a positive role to killing heretics and infidels, especially Muslims occupying the Holy Land.

The historical consciousness allowed Christians to justify conquests and enslavement of whole peoples on the grounds that by drawing them into the Christian orbit, they were in fact blessing them. This historical consciousness was carried over into nationalism as national identification superseded, or at least challenged, Christian identity. National histories justified national crimes just as Christian histories justified Christian ones. Even racism was given historical justification.

A friend recently asked me why Christians had been the most persistent perpetrators of mayhem and enslavement of other peoples. He was looking at the history of the past half-millennium, in which Western Europeans had decimated the people of the Western Hemisphere and pillaged Africa, enslaving millions.

I was taken aback. The question assumed a judgment of historical fact that I wanted to challenge, or at least qualify. I argued that much of this conquest and exploitation had been motivated by national and racial feeling, not by Christianity, which opposed both and had long resisted the use of violence. But the question remained. Although not all of the perpetrators have been Christian believers, the culture from which they came had been profoundly influenced by Christianity, and until very recently most of the perpetrators called themselves Christian.

I would now suggest that historical consciousness was introduced by the Bible and that it is frequently expressed in ways that privilege those who are telling the story. American exceptionalism comes to mind, both as obviously not Christian but also as grounded in a reading of history deeply influenced by the Bible. From the time of Charlemagne, many Christians believed their violence in the conquest of those who were not part of the chosen few was justified. And the rejection of Christianity in the modern world only transferred this feeling of election to Western civilization or one of its national forms.

I do resist, however, presenting only this account of Christian history. If we must take responsibility for many of the most heinous historical crimes, we can also lay claim to some events that are remarkable in their positive promise. Gandhi was inspired by Jesus, and Martin Luther King certainly led a Christian movement. The Truth and Reconciliation Movement in South Africa clearly has Christian roots. These movements are far more directly influenced by distinctive Christian teaching than are the horrible crimes of Christian history. I dare to claim that it was not the service of Abba that led to slaughter and enslavement.

Nevertheless, despite all claims to positive historical contributions, an objective view of the consequences of Christian historical consciousness might lead us to celebrate its recent decline in the West. The study of history now plays a greatly reduced role in our schools, and the Bible is not studied very seriously in our liberal churches. Psychology and social ethics play a much larger role than history in shaping the consciousness even of most Christians.

Unfortunately, the result is not the gain for which we might hope. Historical consciousness always relativizes the present pattern of life and society. Those of us who have historical consciousness understand that the habits and institutions now dominant came into being through particular circumstances. If there are features that we prize, we need to find ways to retain them as circumstances change. If there are features that we see as harmful, we can seek ways to undermine them. We have some sense of which features are inescapable and which are subject to change. We are likely to find that other people who live out of a similar sense of history are ready to work together with us.

Regrettably, education no longer offers a historical perspective on what is happening. Current reality is more likely to be experienced as the inevitable nature of things. We may not like it, but the only realistic option is thought to be to adjust to it. Today, adjusting to the way things are is participation in the massive extinction of species that even threatens the continuance of humans. Whatever harm the historical consciousness has done, today the world needs vast numbers of people to understand our situation in historical perspective, to learn how it can be changed, and to commit ourselves to effecting the needed change.

Needless to say, what is needed is not just any sense of history. A historical consciousness that leads to blaming one class or another, one people or another, one religion or another, and then seeking the villain's destruction, would only worsen the situation. A historical consciousness that depicted modern history as progress effected by science and technology, and that created confidence that these would overcome all dangers, would only reinforce apathy. A historical consciousness that led to expectation of supernatural intervention would have the same effect.

On the other hand, there would be great value in a historical consciousness that opened us to full recognition of the danger we face and how we have come to this situation and to what possible changes we should commit. It could enable us to build on real success stories such as the work of Gandhi and Martin Luther King and the reduction of sexism and racism. If this were combined with a rejection of violence and a sense of solidarity with all humans and with all the forces of life, that would help even more. And if the historical consciousness opened us to fresh ideas and willingness to be used in their implementation, we could recover some realistic hope.

I believe such a story exists and already has some play in our society. It is a story in which Jesus' Abba fits well. Indeed, in the case of Gandhi and King, he stands near the surface. Jesus was Gandhi's inspiration and central to King as well. And Jesus' message of love for enemies, so important to both of them, derives from Jesus' understanding of who Abba is and what Abba wants of us.

2. Abba's Power and Ours

The issue of the nature of power has played a role in previous chapters. It is a matter of great importance in the public affairs with which this chapter deals, and it is central to the understanding of Abba. When we hear that a man is "powerful," we usually think that he is able to make other people do what he wants. Similarly, when we hear that a nation is powerful, we suppose that it is able to compel other nations to do its will. If God is powerful, then, God can compel obedience from both individuals and nations. If God is *all*-powerful, then God can, at will, make anything happen.

I have given reasons from time to time for opposing the notion of divine omnipotence. It makes God responsible for everything that happens. Some who hold that God has the ability to control everything say that God chooses not to use that power so that we may have some power also. But when really terrible situations persist, God's inaction remains incompatible with the idea of God's love.

However, there is a more basic question. More important than the quantity of power attributed to God is the nature of God's power.

When God's power is thought of in conventional terms as ability to control others, the tendency is to affirm that kind of power at the human level as well. Political systems informed by that understanding of divine power tended to centralize top-down control. Emperors and kings played "God" in their domains. Rulers claimed to rule in the name of God, so that obedience to God called for obedience to earthly rulers as well. Humans tyrannized over other animals.

There are, however, other ways of understanding "power." You may note that "power over" is not really creative. It controls some aspects of what has been created. But to bring into being well-informed, committed, sensitive people requires an entirely different kind of power, the kind of power that Abba embodies.

The alternative to coercive power is often thought of as persuasive power. That is an important distinction. But it can be thought of still as limiting the one who is persuaded. Parents may, for example, explain to their children that if they do not eat their vegetables they cannot have dessert. They are not strictly coercing their children, but they are limiting their choices in the effort to "persuade" them to eat vegetables.

To avoid that misunderstanding of "persuasive" power, I suggest that we speak of empowering power and liberating power. If a teacher offers a way of thinking that was not previously available to the student, the freedom of the student to choose is increased. If previously the student was not aware of having any choice in the matter at all and now discovers that she or he does have a choice, this is liberation from bondage. A good education involves a continual expansion of awareness of possibilities not previously imagined. A teacher's ability to stimulate the growth of the student in this way is a greater power than the ability of a bully to force a student to engage in some demeaning act. The power we attribute to Abba is of this superior variety.

In chapter 4 I explained that every event is the outcome of many factors, and that God is just one of these. This means that God never singlehandedly determines exactly what happens. We cannot read God's purposes off of history. Years ago it was pointed out that if we consider God the sole determiner of what happens, then "God is a white racist." In fact, however, God is always confronted by a world, which, to a very large extent, determines its own future. Attributing control to "God" has had terrible consequences. The controlling God has failed.

But this "God" is not the Abba of Jesus. Even if most of what happens in each moment is necessitated by the past, the present is never only the result of that determination. Even in a context of slavery, not everything is settled. Over time, God can sensitize the consciences of some, who then work to abolish slavery. And even while slavery continues, God can call slaves to use what little freedom remains to them to support one another and inwardly to resist the dehumanization inherent in that status.

Abba's exercise of power does not reduce human freedom. It liberates human beings to choose. It does not replace the power of human beings. On the contrary, it empowers them. In short, whereas there are indeed massive powers of compulsion at work in the world, Abba is not one of these.

There are those who identify power so fully with coercive force, that they consider the lack of that kind of power to be weakness. They feel awe and worship before the embodiments of coercive power and treat Abba with contempt. But there are also those who recognize that what is of positive value in the world is not the product of coercive power. Coercive power can determine some aspects of human behavior, but it cannot evoke love or widen horizons or increase understanding. A very different kind of power is required for that. Abba is the one "from whom all blessings flow."

None of this means that a world without necessitation is possible or even desirable. The continuity of things from moment to moment is just as important as whatever elements of spontaneity there may be. Also there are times when we humans need to use coercive force, as in snatching a child away from the path of a speeding car. But this distinction *does* mean that divine power is creative and life-giving, and that we who seek to be responsive to Abba are called primarily to share in its work.

3. Abba's Call for Community

What implications does this have for social life? It would be a mistake to ask for a social theory to be derived from belief in Abba. But we can be sure that what is called for is very different from the currently dominant forms of society.

Our goal, like Jesus' goal, will be so to order society that human life (and, indeed, all life) will flourish. Life flourishes when living things, and we are focusing on people here, are able to express themselves freely. Although it is not possible to avoid compulsion altogether, its role will be secondary. The goal is advanced by providing opportunities to all, and by encouraging and supporting the positive use of these opportunities.

One goal of society is to empower individuals to make their own decisions both freely and wisely. They need the opportunity to make bad choices as well as good ones. They need acceptance even when they make mistakes, but they also need help and guidance and encouragement in the socially beneficial direction. In short, individuals need accepting and nurturing communities, that is, groups of people who liberate, empower, support, and advise one another. These communities should have as much freedom as possible to make their own rules for shared life and organize themselves for responsibility.

The prayer to Abba that Jesus taught his disciples gives some guidance about what constitutes community. We pray that the divine commonwealth will be actualized. To pray for that means that we really want it and that we actualize it as far as we can. We pray for basic necessities, and that means that we do what we can to ensure that these needs are met for all members of the community. We pray for the forgiveness of debts, and that means that we participate as little as possible in the debt system, which works so persistently against personal freedom and flourishing.

In each community, individual persons should feel their shared responsibility for its well-being. To follow the rules on which they have agreed is part of this responsibility. If some of the rules become oppressive rather than furthering the life of the community, they should be changed. The concern is for the common good and rules are in its service.

Within a community, some contribute more than others. Their contribution should be recognized and affirmed. The personal satisfaction and the appreciation of others should be the main reward for outstanding work. If the community wants to reward some workers more than others, and monetary compensation is used, one set of problems may be solved but another is introduced. It will be important to keep the differences small and to focus on other rewards for meritorious achievements.

I do not know of any communities today that are very similar to that of those who followed Jesus during his ministry. I do not know of any that are very similar to the communities of believers brought into being by Paul's missionary work. But let us remember that Paul's communities were different from that of Jesus and were adapted to his situation. Throughout church history the creation of communities continued with greater and lesser success. None, including that of Jesus and those of Paul, were perfect, but imperfection by no means erases their achievements.

Some people have had very little experience of community even in their homes. In contrast, I am fortunate to have experienced communities of many sorts, beginning with the home of my childhood. When I was there as a student, the Divinity School of the University of Chicago was a community of mutual support in wrestling with questions of faith. The "process" movement to which that wrestling gave rise has over the decades since then been a continuing community for me and for a good many others. The Claremont School of Theology, where I taught from 1958 to 1990, also, for me and for many who were part of it, was a community. The Claremont United Methodist Church has been a community. The city of Claremont has also had some of the marks of a community. For a few years, my wife and I lived in a commune with several other couples. It, too, was a community, but it proved much less sustainable than the others I have listed.

It is apparent that the features of community that are possible in our world in different circumstances and institutions differ widely. A city cannot have all of the characteristics of a church. An educational institution cannot have all of the characteristics of a movement. The reverse is also the case. It would be useful to consider the strengths and weaknesses of each of these communities, evaluating them in relation to the real possibilities rather than an ideal description of community as such. However, instead of that I will describe in more detail the community in which I am now particularly fortunate to complete my life.

This community is a retirement home called Pilgrim Place, which is currently celebrating a hundred years of existence. Its residents are mainly people who have worked professionally for some expression of the Christian movement, although the limitation to Christians is now loosened. We are given a lot of control over our individual and corporate lives, and when we realized that we were functioning as an "intentional community," we began to describe ourselves in that way. That means that we work intentionally at reducing our ecological footprints. We also do a great deal to support one another as we age and lose our ability to take care of ourselves.

We do not pool our financial resources, but we do take considerable responsibility for one another in this area as well. Those who can afford to do so contribute extra funds so that those who lack resources to pay their full cost can be aided. In addition, the whole community puts on an annual festival that attracts around ten thousand people and earns about $200,000 for this purpose. The community does not legally guarantee life care, but thus far, once admitted, no one has left because of inability to pay. Who helps and who is helped is not public information and does not affect the status of residents. Those who are well-heeled are no doubt freer to travel and spend extra money on their residences. But we eat the main meal of the day together, we have similar housing, and the difference in lifestyle of the rich and the poor is limited.

Some contribute much more than others to the life of the community, and we are grateful for their leadership and try to express that gratitude. But that appreciation is the only reward. Others are busy with service to the larger community, and this is equally appreciated and affirmed. Still others are much less active, and that is also respected and accepted.

Although this community is more homogenous than many, its members are still quite diverse. In this case, all are senior citizens and many are in various stages of special needs as they age. Some have limited mobility; some are in pain; some are depressed. I do not want to give the impression that everyone is happy all the time. But many comment that they have found here a quality of relationships and security in the support from others that is new for them.

No doubt there is some competition for leadership or recognition, but this plays a very minor role. Positions of leadership are primarily positions of service, for which we are all grateful. Some fail to fulfill their responsibilities and create problems for others, but there is little criticism or judgment. There is dissatisfaction with one matter or another, but to a large extent this can be expressed as a proposal for change that has some chance of receiving attention.

Although there is little explicit talk about how we understand God, most Pilgrims worship Abba. Our deepest commitments are to love one another and work for peace, justice, and sustainability. Some have strong convictions about a God of Love, whereas some have been so affected by the culture of modernity that they try to continue living out of the values of Abba-faith without commitment to "God." I believe that with all its failures and limitations, we are an example of the *basileia theou* into which Jesus called us. I believe there are many communities about which this can be said. I believe that we are called to help more of the societies in which we find ourselves to actualize the divine commonwealth in whatever ways their circumstances allow.

4. Community and Money

Jesus saw the greatest obstacle to realization of the divine commonwealth to be attachment to wealth. The poor could become part of the community easily. For the rich, this was much more difficult. The community of believers that continued in Jerusalem after the crucifixion required that those who joined give all they had to the community. I indicated that Pilgrim Place does not have any requirement of this kind. But I think it has dealt well with what Jesus identified as a crucial issue.

However, if we are hoping to develop a comprehensive society that conforms more to Jesus' hope for community, we need to consider the issue of money thematically. It is not necessary to human life, and some people think that Abba calls for its abolition. As disasters occur with increasing intensity and frequency, money will, at least temporarily, assume less importance. After disasters, a society typically organizes itself to meet the essential needs of all based on the availability of workers and supplies, without requiring payment. Money plays little role. It may be that in the future this kind of community will be in many places the most that can be hoped for.

However, while appreciating this possibility, we need to recognize that much that we have all come to prize cannot be realized in such communities. We prize our abilities to choose which goods we acquire and which we forego. We prize the ability to engage in complex professional activities. We want productive businesses and markets and specialized educational institutions. We cannot have these things without a medium of exchange, and whatever medium is used, we can call money.

The problem is that once money exists in any form, it becomes highly desirable and even necessary for survival. Accordingly, its possession gives great power. In Genesis we read how Joseph established himself in the court of pharaoh by showing him how to use his wealth to turn the free people of Egypt into slaves of the pharaoh. To avoid starvation they had to obtain food from the pharaoh. For this they pledged their property and finally themselves. Since they could not repay the pharaoh in any other way, he took possession of their property and then of their persons.

Frequently in the ancient world, the prosperous loaned money to their needy neighbors and acquired their property and their persons.

They turned societies of free farmers into slave societies. While a few individuals prospered, the society as a whole deteriorated. When a country was attacked and the king raised an army of free farmers, he had their support, since they had something to defend. He could not count on much from an army of slaves. For this and other reasons, kings from time to time declared a jubilee, giving freedom to slaves and returning to them their land. The jubilee was affirmed in Israel, although we do not know how often it actually occurred. Jesus taught us to pray for the jubilee, when we ask for the forgiveness of debts.

What made debts so often unpayable was interest. Debtors had to pay back more than they borrowed. This was often not possible. The Hebrew Scriptures forbid Jews to charge interest of other Jews, and in Christian Europe, Christians could not charge interest of other Christians. Sadly, this created a situation in which Jews became the moneylenders and thus the financiers of Europe. Given the evils of the debt system, it is not surprising that Jews were hated.

The problems of individuals are compounded at the national level. Nations borrow money at interest and cannot repay. We have just seen the power this gives financial institutions over nations in the case of Greece. In the United States also, we have learned that no matter how corrupt the large financial institutions become, they are "too big to fail"; so they have nothing to fear from government. Their enormous wealth gives them enormous power.

Obviously we cannot look to Jesus' prayer to Abba to provide knowledge of how to organize our economic and financial life. But I have felt called, as one who seeks to follow Jesus, to think about this. Can we organize our society in a way that avoids the debt system and reduces the lure of wealth? And I think we can.

I see two steps that would move us closer to the divine commonwealth for which we pray. Both of these steps are actualized in some countries, so this is not fantasy. First, we need to understand that for the most part, money *is* debt. It is a promise to pay. It is created when you borrow money from the bank. The bank promises to make the money available to you and opens an account. Opening the account does not require money; so it is often said that the bank creates the money out of thin air. You will then owe the bank the amount of the loan plus interest. When you pay it off, the account is liquidated. But because you also pay interest, the bank now has money. For you to have acquired the money to pay the interest, someone else must have borrowed the money. Otherwise the total money supply would not suffice for people to pay interest. In order that interest be paid, the money supply must increase.

Your borrowing is not likely by itself to greatly affect the economy. But in the case of another borrower, governments, it does. Actually, if governments did not spend more than they take back in taxes, the money supply would often not increase sufficiently to keep the system afloat. So in many countries, such as the United States, the government borrows a lot of money. Since the payment of interest adds to the budget, the annual deficits tend to get larger and larger.

Some countries have realized that they do not need to borrow money from banks. Rather than have the banks create the money and charge them interest, the government can directly create its own money. It can create money by paying for infrastructure, for example. If the treasury took over from the Federal Reserve, it could create the money to pay off the debt and end governmental interest payments. This would reduce both the revenue and the political power of the private financial institutions.

If a country has debts that it must pay in a currency other than its own, this solution to its problems is not available. This was the case with Greece, for example, and has been the problem for many Third World countries.

If the United States chose to make the profits from money-creation available to the government, it could take a second step. It could follow the example of some European countries in guaranteeing sufficient services and money that no one will have to borrow money for necessities. This takes the worst of the sting out of the debt system. It leaves open the possibility of borrowing to start a business or to buy a yacht. We may risk the loss of much, but our basic needs are not at stake. The love of money may still prevent many from becoming part of the divine community, but social pressures in that direction will not be as strong.

5. Communities of Communities

We get even less help from Jesus with respect to other political issues. He makes it very clear that our supreme loyalty is to Abba, not to any political power. Paul reaffirms this but also emphasizes that Christians should be model citizens. But neither Jesus nor Paul saw any point in discussing how the Roman Empire should organize itself.

Over the centuries the situation has changed. During the Middle Ages Christian ideas were important in structuring the political order. This order rejected slavery and asserted that everyone had some rights. Gradually this developed, so that some Christians began claiming that every child of God had equal rights. Remarkably some Christians combined language of that kind with the acceptance of slavery! And even leading political thinkers continued to subordinate human rights to property rights.

Once the question of how political life should be organized is raised, Christians have every reason to enter. Although they cannot deduce a theory from Jesus' teaching, they can be clear that Jesus' attitude toward wealth and community does not support the priority of property over human beings. Clearly in God's eyes the poor are as important as the rich, and any political theory that purports to be based on the prophetic tradition of Israel or Jesus' modification thereof must consider its effect on the poorest and most oppressed. Also, it should encourage and be based on positive relations among people, their mutual support and concern. In short, political units like social ones should have as many of the characteristics of community as possible. I will not discuss the nature of community further.

The political question that I have not considered thus far is the relationship among communities. This can include the relationship between political and religious communities, and many other matters of this sort. But at this point I will attend only to the relationship of geographically based communities to one another.

Again, we can look to Jesus' Abba only for very general principles. Clearly human flourishing cannot occur if each community feels threatened by all the others and devotes itself to protection against the others. Worse still, some will decide that the best defense is an offense. Tribes and city-states all too often fight one another until control over them is centralized in a kingdom or empire. Abba surely does not desire either warring states or imperial centralization of power. What is needed is a community of communities and then a community of communities of communities.

In more standard political language, this means some kind of voluntary federation based on the assumption that surrendering some powers to a central agency benefits all. In the church system, individual congregations usually feel that they can accomplish their mission better if they share many projects through centralized agencies. The states in the United States often still describe themselves as "sovereign," but of course they depend on one army to defend them and one government to make many decisions. The United States and other nations are also organized into the United Nations. The idea of a community of communities of communities is not wholly fanciful. But it would be hard to celebrate many of them in their present form.

Of course, the present global order is very far from realizing the ideal. Some nations do have a sense of community with some others. But all too often their sense of community is partly stimulated by viewing still other nations as threats. Too often, also, community is really a subordination of some to others. The United Nations assembly has never been given the power it would require to carry out its mandates.

Here, too, while the view that communities should relate to one another in larger communities can be derived from our general understanding of Abba's purposes in the world, the best distribution of power to the various levels of community cannot be derived from the general principles alone. Trial and error are always part of positive historical developments. And the system that works best in one historical situation will not work well in another.

Christians often remind each other that in developing political proposals they should take human sinfulness seriously. This is certainly true. Even the best structures can be used for the benefit of some and the exploitation of others. But the emphasis on human sinfulness is too often used by the privileged to support the unjust *status quo* and to put down proposals for positive change.

We do better to identify critical features of "human nature" and see how they operate. I have come to the conclusion that, in terms of the ordering of society, a crucial feature is the "we/they" distinction. Few people are naturally entirely selfish. That kind of individualism is a product of social disintegration. Most people grow up in families and larger communities, and most people identify themselves and their interests with these larger groups. This is, in itself, positive.

However, typically this small community intensifies its internal unity by distinguishing itself from other communities in competitive ways. Sometimes this is friendly and healthy competition, but it can also easily take on another character. For private political advantage, politicians often demonize the other, whoever that may be.

I have spoken of communities of communities. These are communities that band together in mutual support. Often they are motivated to support one another by viewing still other communities as threats. The challenge to organizing the world into communities of communities of communities of communities is that at this limit the "we" has no "they" against which to organize. Is it possible to organize against famine and war? Perhaps. But perhaps this asks of the human emotional structure abilities it lacks.

My hopeful argument is to show the extent to which people have at times followed Jesus. He taught us to love our enemies, so that love includes "them" among "us." Gandhi and King were able to organize large groups of people to adopt this strategy. Perhaps, just perhaps, if we can draw more people into the service of Abba, what appears as naïve idealism can play a larger role in human history. I commend such hope rather than simply acquiescing to the need for group enemies in order to transcend individual selfishness.

6. Abba, Francis, and the Global Crisis

The global crisis has been part of the background of everything in this book. How could it not be so? We are living in the midst of an extinction of classic proportions, of a change of climate that could make much of the planet uninhabitable, of the death of the oceans, of the poisoning and erosion of the soil, of genetic change even of the human body and our reproductive systems. Surely, we cannot ignore all this!

Does belief in God help us in this context? Many forms of belief in God provide some kind of reassurance, but some of it is simply misleading. Those who assert that God will not allow humanity to destroy itself are appealing to a God who does not exist. Those who think God is punishing most of us for our sins, but will snatch the good ones and take them to heaven, poison the social and spiritual atmosphere and do nothing about the real problems.

Some of the reassurance is right and true. Abba is with us even as we destroy ourselves. But if this reassurance leads to nothing but moving ahead along established lines, it may do more harm than good. For some, it seems, the turn to prayer and meditation is an escape from responsibility and action in the world.

I am convinced, however, that renewing faith in Abba will direct us to the world Abba loves and to the effort to save what can be saved and to build on the wreckage something of lasting value. Fortunately, we who turn to Abba will not be alone in these efforts. There are many who have rejected God for good reasons but still care deeply about the future of humanity and all life and who know that we cannot save ourselves with the thinking and policies that have led us into our crisis. There are Jews and Muslims and Hindus and Buddhists who will not speak of Jesus' Abba, but who, in the eyes of those who do, are doing Abba's will. As Jesus is reported to have said, it is not those who say "Lord, Lord," but those who serve Abba in fact with whom we can share our efforts.

I have noted above that for Jesus the great choice is between serving Abba and serving wealth. The decision to serve Abba corresponds with the choice of LIFE. To choose LIFE in a culture that does not value it or even believe that it really exists is a daring and costly move. Jesus chose to serve Abba, and he was crucified. Abba deals with us gently, but Abba calls for action that is not always gentle and is often roughly treated by those servants of wealth who rightly recognize the servants of Abba as a threat.

I am writing this in the joyful glow of the publication of a great encyclical. Pope Francis, like the saint whose name he took, is a worshiper of Abba. As a good worshiper of Abba he addresses himself to those who serve LIFE by other names, as well as to fellow Christians who have often served idols instead of Abba. Jesus stood in the prophetic tradition, as do all who serve Abba, and Pope Francis stands with him, speaking the truth in love. But the servants of wealth seem not much moved by love. They rightly hear that they are called to repentance, that is, *metanoia*, a change of mind, but they do not want to change their way of thinking. We may be sure that great quantities of their wealth will be spent on "spin," to distract the public from the simple truth, and raise all sorts of questions that are designed to turn the truth into just one political opinion among others.

But this may be a new day. The servants of wealth have silenced truth thus far in the media and in the universities. Thousands of us have experienced their ability to prevent the real issues from receiving serious attention. But they may have met their match! Perhaps even in defending themselves they will have to place the real issues before the public. Lies love darkness, for if they are openly discussed, the positions of those who worship wealth cannot be sustained. Once the light is brought to bear on them, they crumble.

Consider the commitment of the servants of wealth to economic growth. We live in a world that is demonstrably consuming resources and using "sinks," that is, nature's capacity to recycle our wastes, unsustainably, which means we cannot continue consuming at the present rate. To advocate policies that increase the overuse of resources and sinks is in the strictest sense insane. To notice this does not require any special knowledge. It only requires that you take the risk of speaking the truth in a world that is owned by those who prefer lies.

If we can change the political discourse so that this simple commonsense principle can be publicly discussed, the defenders of increasingly unsustainable behavior cannot win. We can instead have public discussions of how to meet the needs of all and provide jobs for all in the process of shifting toward sustainable practices. There are many excellent ideas available to guide us in this discussion—once a forum is provided. The work of Pope Francis may make this possible and might give sensible guidance to the discussion.

Let us not deceive ourselves. The enemies of LIFE have already ensured that millions will die. It is too late to prevent terrible suffering. The ocean levels will continue to rise. Storms will grow worse. The ocean will produce less food for us. Deserts will grow. Famines will cause many to starve. Masses of people will migrate in quest of shrinking supplies of arable land. Violence will increase.

But, perhaps, instead of manufactured arguments about whether this is even happening, we can work together to reduce the damage and to mitigate the suffering. Perhaps we can begin to create a different system of food production. Perhaps we can seriously discuss alternatives to the debt system, to our private financial institutions, to our neoliberal economic theories. Perhaps we can abandon the absurdity of value-free scholarship and enlist our universities in serving a desperately needful world and in preparing students to do so as well. Perhaps we can ask how the people who are governed can have a voice in the decisions that determine their fate.

If so, Jesus' Abba will be pleased, and we will all join in celebrating the work of Pope Francis. And perhaps, just perhaps, more people will join him in the worship of Abba.

Postscript

The purpose of this book is to propose that it is time for thoughtful Christians to free themselves from acquiescence to the late modern worldview. My conviction is that the biblical worldview in general, and the worldview of Jesus and Paul in particular, is superior. Of course, there are many respects in which their worldview is out of date. But bringing it up to date is much easier and more fruitful than trying to make the modern worldview adequate to our needs.

We certainly have a great deal of knowledge about astronomy today that is far more accurate than the beliefs that prevailed in New Testament times. But adjusting to that information is no threat to the basic insights of Jesus or Paul. We know now that the world is composed of quantum events, a view that is vastly different from ideas in the minds of any New Testament writer. But their worldview was basically one that gave primacy to events. That events characterize the world at microscopic levels is not an uncongenial idea, whereas the modern world is not able to assimilate it. And above all, the idea that events are both subjective and objective would pose no problem to the ancients, whereas the moderns have to deny it, conceal it, or treat it as an anomaly.

I have focused on what is central for Jesus, the reality and purposes of Abba. I have wanted to show that belief in Abba makes a lot of sense today. Of course, I have not proved the existence of Abba; indeed, it is not really possible to prove the existence of anything. I cannot prove that I exist, but we know much that we cannot prove. We cannot prove that there were any events before the present moment. How could we do so? But I for one do not doubt that many things have happened, and I doubt that you are seriously doubtful.

Although we cannot prove anything, we can disprove a good many things. We can disprove the indivisibility of what we still call atoms, named when we thought they were indivisible. Science has disproved the astronomy generally accepted in New Testament times. It has disproved the idea that the world is just six thousand years old.

I believe we *can* disprove some beliefs about God as well. For example, the systematic implications of the belief that God is all-powerful and the belief that God is all-beneficent contradict each other, and their combination is incompatible with the historical facts. It is very sad when those who consider themselves followers of Jesus spend their time defending ideas that are indefensible and are not found in the Bible. The idea that the Bible is inerrant is another belief that is easily disproved. So is the idea that Jesus and Paul were supporters of what are today called "family values."

The basic argument of this book is that, although many ideas associated with God and Christian faith have been disproved, Jesus' teaching about Abba has not. On the contrary, it is coherent with our experience and responds well to the needs of the world in our day. It can be tested against personal experience. I commend it enthusiastically.

For my part, I strive to be a faithful disciple of Jesus. There are those who follow Jesus without sharing his belief in Abba. I admire them, but I am convinced that the effort to follow Jesus while ignoring his Abba has a tragic character. It usually results from being socialized into a culture and a way of thinking that is not deserving of commitment. I am convinced that a much deeper and more joyful faithfulness is possible if we seek to relate to Abba as Jesus did. I commend a faithfulness to Jesus that shares Jesus' confidence in the love and empowering power of Abba.